BROKEN
Heals

TIFFANY YOUNG

Copyright © 2020 by Tiffany Young

All rights reserved.

No part of this publication may be reproduced, distributed, or transmitted in any form or by any means, including photocopying, recording, or other electronic or mechanical methods, without the prior written permission of the publisher, except in the case of brief quotations embodied in critical reviews and certain other non-commercial uses permitted by copyright law. For permission requests, contact the publisher.

ISBN: 978-1-7332980-3-2

CONTENTS

Chapter 1 1

Chapter 2 5

Chapter 3 9

Chapter 4 13

Chapter 5 17

Chapter 6 21

Chapter 7 27

Chapter 8 35

Chapter 9 45

Chapter 10 53

Chapter 11 59

Chapter 12 71

Chapter 13 79

Chapter 14 87

Chapter 15 95

Chapter 16 107

Chapter 17 123

Chapter 18 139

Chapter 19 151

CHAPTER 1.

"There is no greater agony than bearing an untold story inside you."

– Maya Angelou

As Christians we were taught to be charitable, love, forgive, and judge not. The bible says that Love is patient, love is kind. It does not boast, is not rude or mean. It doesn't wish for bad things to happen to others. The people who are the most difficult to love are the people that need love the most. We were taught to believe in the possibility of all things because we serve a supernatural God who can make anything, and everything happen. I believed the world was mostly good and anything bad was surely not of God. It had to come from the devil. God does not hurt people, but he does allow people to be hurt in order to teach that person a lesson. Ultimately our fate would not be left up to us because we had no control over it. When bad things happen, thank God for that which you do not understand and trust that it all for your own good – or for the good of someone else.

Sometimes bad things happen and there is nothing you can do about it. If something bad did happen, you must pray about it and wait for God to respond. God always responds with either a yes, no, or maybe. That's when you pray the serenity prayer. You ask God to grant you the serenity to accept the things that you do not understand, the courage to change the things that you can change, and the wisdom to know the difference between the two.

Whenever I felt alone, I was comforted by the story of the "Footprints in the Sand". It was about a man that was walking with God and questioned why there was only one set of footprints whenever he went through hard times. God responded and said that it was during those times that he was being carried. The footprints were God's footprints not the man's.

Daddy made sure that God was at the center of everything we did. We prayed without ceasing, just as the word of God commands. "A family that prays together, stays together", he exclaimed. He would always answer phone calls with a cheerful, "Praise God, Hello". Daddy had the most kids so he would always win the prize on friends and family day. He loved bragging about his kids, and we all loved making him proud. The disadvantage of having a preacher for a dad is that we were often the subject of his sermons. That whole, 'what happens in this house stays in this house' apparently was null and void once the Lord tells him to tell our business.

"I had to whoop my baby girl's butt the other day for stealing peanut butter cookies out the refrigerator." I can still hear them gasping like they'd never stolen cookies or candy when they were a child. "She asked to play hide and go seek so she can hide in the closet and eat em'. She came out the closet with peanut butter breath. Left all the evidence behind."

The ladies of the church exclaim, "No She didn't, Deacon"

"YES, SHE DID!"

I wanted to disappear.

I loved singing in the choir. They let the children sing on youth Sunday and I would sing my song, "This Little Light of Mine". You haven't heard the song until you heard me sing it. Daddy remixed the lyrics and the tempo, gave it some bass – something we can dance to. He always said his daughters would make a record someday. That day never came. Two of my favorite childhood gospel songs by Luther Barnes were "Bring Back the Joy", and "I'm Still Holding On". I knew the words and I sang them as if I could relate. Perhaps I did on a more immature Christian level that matched my perception. As I experienced more throughout life the lyrics of those songs had more significance. One served as a beacon of hope and reminder to be strong.

"They said I wouldn't make it. They said I wouldn't be here today. They said I'd never amount to anything. But I'm glad to say that I'm on my way and I'm going more and more each day."

"You see when I was young, I gave God my hand and I told him to lead the way though the road has been rough, and the going's been mighty tough still I ain't going nowhere I'm right here to stay. Though I've been talked about and oh I've been criticized I had to wipe many tears from my eyes but I'm still holding on to his hand."

The other would bring me to tears in those times when I couldn't feel God's presence near me. It was usually because I was lost. I'd strayed or lost faith. It'd hard to drown out the darkness and the distractions of the enemy when your spirit is weak.

"Lately I've been thinking, about the way my life has changed. I've got to find a way to start all over again. There's a question in my heart. What can make my life anew? I want back that inner peace that only comes from knowing you. There was a time when I felt closer but now, I feel so far away. So now I'm reaching out to you, Lord and this is my prayer today.

I could feel your hold spirit but somehow things are quite the same. All I want is to be happy and to be cared for by you. I want to be your humble servant and let my light come shining through."

Gospel music can inspire people and move them no matter where they are in life or what they might be going through or survived. It lifts any mood and encourage strength. This was especially true for me. I loved singing in the choir.

Every summer we attended Vacation Bible School where we studied and rehearsed the books of the bible. We were rewarded for memorizing scriptures, biblical characters and everything from the Old Testament to the New Testament. I could quote scriptures like nobody's business and act out every one of the stories of the bible by the time I was eight years old. It made daddy proud. I loved making my daddy proud.

My imagination was shaped by a combination of fairytales and biblical stories of miracles. The course of events in my life would only add conflict to these beliefs rather than confirm them. It was hard for me to separate real life from the fictional characters in the books I loved to read.

Church was an all-day event on Sundays. Sunday school was followed by a 1 to 2-hour praise and worship service before the Pastor preached his sermon. Praise and worship was my favorite part of every service especially on youth Sunday. I have always been comforted by gospel music. To me it was like being wrapped in God's love and the singing voices of the angels that surround me.

Church had a lot of rules. The ushers were the enforcers of these rules. Don't talk when it's not time to talk like during prayer. Don't walk when it's not time to walk. Don't sit when it's time to shout. When you shout it's not real unless you fall out. At least that's what I understood from the many pinches to my arm whenever I broke the rules.

After church, when we got done praying and crying and being slain in the spirit, the members would be out in the parking lot selling dinners while gossiping, cussing and smoking cigarettes - all the things that were not "of God".

I was a child consumed by my faith, optimism and hope. I was gullible and naive to believe the world was mostly good. Although it's what I believed, that simply was not my experience and eventually things didn't make sense to me anymore. I witnessed hypocrisy at the highest of levels. The same people that taught me scriptures from God's word were the same ones I'd see getting a little too familiar with my daddy. It was hard to ignore the ugliness of the way people treated each other. They'd put on a Christian smile while harboring wickedness in their hearts. Still I felt obligated to please both my father on earth and my Heavenly father. I decided I'm not going to be like those people in the church. I'm going to be the good in the world. I'd always do the right thing, no matter what.

CHAPTER 2.

My mom was going to school for nursing. She was an example of what the bible refers to as a wholesome woman. Petite little lady with curves and legs that commanded attention. You would not think she'd given birth six times, but she did. By 35 years of age my mother had given birth to four girls and two boys. Our family genes must've included all the best kinds of collagen and elastin.

My mother never cussed. No matter how angry she was she had control over her tongue and only spoke in love. The occasional darn it, dang it, and calling Daddy a blind black bastard was about the closest she came to profanity. Maybe a little eye roll here and there as an added measure so you'd know she meant business. Even then it was always awkward.

For the better part of my primary years, we lived in low-income housing apartments. She made it feel like Eden. To us it was just our way of life. We were happy. Everyone around us was in the same situation but they appeared miserable and unhappy. Money was always low, but she never really showed signs of worry or struggle. She never let us see her cry. Whenever our electricity got disconnected, we'd light a few candles in the house and tell spooky stories with little flashlights attached to our chin. For food we would make sugar sandwiches or sandwiches out of whatever else was around. I can still taste the strong flavor of the government cheese. We couldn't afford food all the time so we would often visit food banks where they were giving away free food.

My dad was rarely ever home. When he did come home, we were already in bed asleep, but we could hear them arguing and then it wasn't long before he'd be gone again. Despite the arguing I thought my mom and dad had a loving relationship. I believed this based on my observation of other couples in our immediate family and at the church. We could hear them arguing but we never knew what they were arguing about and we wouldn't dare get up to get a closer look at the action. In the happy times he was always kissing on her and grabbing her butt. It's no wonder they ended up with six kids together.

Daddy had a bad drug habit and would take money from Mama and items from the house that he could sell to get his fix. Today it was the microwave. He and I never talked about what lead to his addiction, but I always thought it probably had something to do with his discharge from the military. Or perhaps he was discharged from the military because of his addiction. He told us that he was medically discharged because of his sickle cell disease. He was born with beta thalassemia, an incurable genetic disorder of the blood, that causes the red blood cells to change shapes. He wasn't expected to live a long life and was told he would never be able to procreate. His disease caused him to be in a lot of pain all the time. There is no cure so whenever he would have a crisis the only thing doctors could do was try to make him comfortable and minimize the pain with drugs. In hindsight, maybe that's what lead to his drug addiction. Maybe he was searching for a way to medicate the pain without pharmaceutical drugs. Or a way to forget his painful reality even for a moment. The causticness of that theory is that it was often the street drugs that triggered his sickle cell crisis. Mama tried to stop him sometimes. She tried to get him to quit but she never could, so she tried her best to love him through it. She loved him. Opening the door to our home and her heart hoping that this time the man standing there would be the man that she fell in love with.

Whenever Daddy would have a crisis he would lay in bed in cry for hours and even days. My mom would find herself taking care of both her husband and their six kids. We knew when his pain was unbearable because he would cry out for his mama. One of my most vivid memories of my daddy in crisis was when he asked me to rub him down with green alcohol. My mom would be busy with the babies. I'd done this countless time before because these crises happened often. It broke my heart to see my superhero dad curled up in the fetal position and hear him crying out in pain. I wanted to take his pain away. Rubbing his body with green alcohol seemed to bring him some relief. It helped to dull the pain. Daddy turned over on his stomach. He was naked. Our family had gotten comfortable with a lot of things some people would consider bizarre or abnormal family behavior. Whenever my dad was in crisis, he would be uncomfortable with any clothing against his skin so he would lay in bed naked. This time I don't know if I was trying to cover more of his body at one time or if I was just being extra for no good reason, but I poured too much. The alcohol ran down his spine and in between the crack of his butt. In that moment, the burning in his butt was more significant than sickle shaped blood cells running through his veins. He jumped up out of the bed and ran around the room jumping up and down. I stood there puzzled and confused not knowing what to do. I simply didn't think a butt could burn.

My mother was on the PTA at school and chaperoned every field trip. Whenever daddy came home sober it was like Disneyland. He was reckless fun. Piggyback rides with three kids on his back, hide-and-seek that lead to the forbidden corners of our apartment. I was small enough to fit under the couch. One time it took them so long to find me, Daddy got scared. He threatened to whoop me if I didn't come out from my hiding place. I immediately complied.

Daddy loved to sing. He made up a country song entirely about his "booty hole" itching.

"My booty hole itchin' my booty hole itchin' my booty hole itchin' bad. I think I'd better scratch it; I think I'd better scratch it; I think I'd better scratch it bad." We'd always crack up when Daddy sang that song. Or when he and mama would have a friendly debate about the proper term for gas. Daddy said, *"poot* and *fart"*, mama said *"flatulate"*. In either case potty talk was hilarious and daddy was all for it all the time. He would let out the loudest most disgusting rounds of thunderous gas and leave anyone there in the fumes. That was the best. As he began to outgrow his addiction the song that we attached to many of our childhood memories of dad would serve as a reminder of a time in his life that he didn't make the healthiest choices. A time he wanted to forget. To us, it was our fondest memories of time we shared with our dad.

After baby number six, my parents finally decided on a tubal ligation despite protests from Daddy who always wanted a big family. Apparently, to him, after 6 kids our family still wasn't big enough, but he did digress.

After years of living with his addiction Daddy finally gave up drugs. At the time, to me, it felt like it happened overnight. As my perception matured, I now know this was not the case. It was a daily battle. He was fighting with himself and his demons. The drugs would drown out the noise make thing quiet again but now he'd have to face these demons on his own. He did it. With constant prayer and trusting in his faith, he did it. ,After that he became a lot more involved with our family. He'd eventually grown tired of how the drugs and alcohol was affecting him and made the changes on his own. He was looking good and had a lot more energy which was a bonus for us. I first fell in love with horses the day Daddy took us horseback riding at Tradewinds Park. I was about 6 years only. We would drive out to Alligator Alley almost once a month to go fishing. He taught me how to bait the hook. I was never grossed out by the worms and the bugs. I loved it. I loved spending time with him.

He started cooking more too. We set up bird traps outside to catch our dinner. I never actually saw any of the birds we caught before he fried them up. Nor did I see the wild rabbit he served at dinner from time to time. They all tasted just like chicken.

He burned down the kitchen in a couple of apartments causing Mama to get evicted and us practically homeless until we found another place to live. The first apartment he burned down was while frying French fries on the stove. That was the day I learned that putting water on a grease fire only causes the fire to spread. The other times he was making my favorite sweet snack. We called it coconut candy. Daddy would pick a coconut from underneath the coconut tree in Grandma's back yard and cut it up into pieces. On the stove he cooked it with brown sugar, butter, ginger and some other ingredients I never paid an attention to. I later learned that it was a popular Jamaican delicacy called coconut drop. There was nothing delicate about the way the kitchen went up in flames that day.

CHAPTER 3.

"Anyone who has ever struggled with poverty knows how extremely expensive it is to be poor."

James Baldwin

Growing up as the third eldest of 6 kids had its benefits. You were never alone. Our apartments were usually two-bedroom apartments. The kids all slept in one room and we knew to never enter the adult room without permission. At any moment there could be a bonding moment or a brawl. We shared everything – the bed, our clothes and our food. Almost all my clothes were handed down from my big sister or older cousins – even my mom. Yes, once upon a time I had to wear my mom's shoes to school because we couldn't afford to buy me some new ones. I would not have had a problem with them if they weren't her work shoes and 3 sizes too big. I had to wear three pairs of socks and stuff tissue inside just to keep them from flopping.

Birthday celebrations were contingent upon mama's bank balance and her willingness to sacrifice one of the bills. Angel, Dee and Man-Man all celebrated their birthdays during tax season. They'd usually receive nice gifts and even birthday parties. The money was all gone by the time my birthday came around in June. Somehow my mom always managed a miracle for my baby brother's birthday which was just 8 days before mine. On my birthday she was always broke. Then my baby sister's birthday came around in July and she'd always be celebrated because she shared a birthday with my maternal grandmother. There was a silver lining. I found some comfort in being happy for my siblings whenever they got celebrated. It meant I'd get some cake too which was almost as important as getting presents, right? I hid the fact that it made me feel insignificant and unloved. Disappointment grew with each passing year until I stopped hoping this year would be the year, I'd get a cake with my name on it. A celebration in honor of me.

The holidays for us consisted of purchasing a Christmas tree with whatever money Mama was able to scrape up. We decorated it with various things of sentiment such as assorted photographic memories of friends and family and artwork we'd made in school. These were hung on the tree as ornaments. We used string lined with Kix cereal and popcorn instead of lights so we wouldn't run up the light bill. Under the tree wrapped as gifts were boxes of things we needed like socks and underwear. Occasionally, we would get something good like my Spanish Speaking Baby Alive Doll, depending on which bill my mom had sacrificed that month. Most of the time it would be a board game, or something labeled *to The Young Family from Santa*.

I always wanted to learn Spanish, so this Hispanic baby doll was the best gift ever. She became my best friend, but you couldn't tell by how dirty she was. I carried her everywhere I went and annoyed everyone with my limited Spanish speaking abilities. I'd jumble up all the Spanish words I knew into a sentence. It didn't matter if they made sense. What mattered is that I was speaking a language than no one else knew but me. She taught me how to count to 10 in Spanish and common beginner greetings with, "Hola, Como esta, Muy Bien, gracias" set to repeat. My Spanish is God awful now. Even after taking Spanish courses in college and living in multicultural South Florida, I did not retain the second language. It's limited to those same basic salutations and common phrases.

We had lots of friends that would come over and play with us. Our village was large. Neighbors and neighborhood kids stuck together and looked out for each other. My mom being so involved with the PTA was well known by the other moms and the teachers at school. Everyone knew the

Young family. My older brother would always get into the most trouble. He'd test boundaries and cause mischief anywhere we went. He thought he wouldn't get caught. I don't think he was thinking at all. Not even when he broke his hip doing a balancing act on the wooden gate around the park. He had to be in a body cast all summer.

TIFFANY YOUNG

CHAPTER 4.

"Hey, Black Child do you know who you are? Who you really are? Do you know you can be what you want to be if you try to be what you can be?"

– Useni Eugene Perkins, Hey Black Child

I stood 2 feet above her watching her sleeping peacefully in her car seat. She was adorable. Her shiny jet-black curls fell perfectly onto her melanin covered forehead skin. She was my new baby sister that had been riding around in my mom's tummy for what at the time seemed to me like my entire life. There were four of us already. Dee, Man-Man, Me and Gucci. Gucci wasn't even 2-year-old yet, I was 4, Man-Man was 5 and Dee was 6 years old. I was perfectly fine with having a baby brother, we didn't need her too. She was so cute though. I didn't like her.

"I should bite her", must've been my thoughts at the time. That's assuming I was thinking any deeper than whatever jealousy I was feeling at the time. I didn't expect her reaction to be so dramatic. You would think I set the girl on fire. Her screams were that of a banshee wailing warns of an impending death on our house. Like I was trying to kill her. Hurt her, yes, but not kill her.

Obviously my 4-year-old mind had not thought this through thoroughly. I'd reacted off pure impulse and resentment of my new baby sister and now I must get her to be quiet before the lights go out on me. Mama would surely be coming, and she would be livid. I knew I only had a few seconds. Quickly I grabbed her pacifier and thrusted it between her tiny lips without a second thought. I heard footsteps running, here she comes. Although I tried to pretend that I was nothing but a hero big sister coming to the rescue of my screaming baby sister - who was screaming for no reason at all – I didn't think to hide the evidence of my crime. My mom immediately noticed the deep imprint of toddler teeth embedded in my sister's wrist. It was still wet and everything.

I thought I'd been hit by lightning, but it was just my mom's enormous hammer hand thrusting against my back. I saw darkness, just as I'd anticipated, followed by a flash of light. I think it took a while for me to cry because she'd knocked me into next week.

Growing up in a big family teaches humility. As the third eldest I had to be enormously selfless. We had to make a lot of sacrifices. Food was distributed youngest to eldest. You never take the last of anything. If you needed to go #2, you had better ask if anyone needed to pee first or it was World War 3 in the house.

At a very young age I was casted with the tasks of taking care of my younger siblings. My chores included babysitting, bathing the younger kids, serving dinner, being accountable and making adult decisions. It made me a nurturer but subsequently I always felt responsible for other people both in and outside of my family. I always considered other people's feelings. My own feelings, what made me comfortable, mattered very little.

Having a big family meant any moment could be made into a party. There were six of us. Pillow fights, dance contests, talent shows, and made up games were frequent visitors in our home. It also meant a fight could break out at any time.

We spent a lot of time with our cousins who were more like siblings to us. Either we were at their house or they were at ours. Mama often depended on the help of her family. With six kids and no car we'd have to walk or catch the city bus everywhere we needed to go. I imagine mama looked like mother goose walking up the street with her children following close behind her like ducks.

We called ourselves the Nutty Buddy Gang – like the ice cream. Had a theme song and everything and would sing it every day with auntie Lyn on the way to buy Nutty Buddys from the corner store. We would sing the song just because. Aunty Lyn had 5 kids of her own, but they all had different fathers. My eldest cousin Joanna, then John, Eric, Tia, and Isaiah. Joanna was a few years older than the rest of us. She was too mature for the Nutty Buddy Gang. John, my favorite cousin, was right behind her in age but he was always ready for some ice cream and some fun. The rest of us clowned around insistently.

Akia and I were closest in age. She was five months older than me, but we were in the same grade. Her father was my father's uncle. My paternal grandmother was her aunt. We didn't share any friends. Akia hung around with a different crowd of girls. The kind I tried staying far away from. In middle school she would get into fights after school on a regular basis – almost weekly.

Eric wore big prescription eyeglasses but had the biggest heart. He would give his last piece of food to anyone who asks. If he only had a dollar and the ice cream truck came onto our street, he would always share his food. His mental health would lead to homelessness as an adult after Aunty Lyn moved away to California with her husband James.

John was older too, but he was big cousin. He always looked out for his family. Nobody could mess with us and get away with it. I was his favorite cousin too. I felt safe when he was around. He got into a lot of trouble too and was in and out of jail for one reason or another. I would write letters to him telling him about anything and everything that was happening in my life. I would tell him how much I miss him, and I wished he was home. As the years passed, he would spend more time away than at home. Seasons changed. We grew apart.

Isaiah was younger than me but around the same age as Angel and Tootie. To me he was my annoying little cousin just as much as Tootie and Angel were my annoying little sisters.

My maternal grandmother, aunts and uncles would pitch in to help mama out but not without talking about what they did and how much they had to do. It was common that I'd hear my aunt on the phone with my grandma or one of my uncles taking about how dirty we were when they took my mom to the laundry mat. Or about how they had to cook for us, and they'd exaggerate suggesting we were so hungry that we ate up all the food. We weren't that starved; we were just greedy.

There were times when on occasion our light would get disconnected or our or our water would get turned off because we couldn't pay the bill. Even in those cases we never went hungry. There was a Wendy's Restaurant that was walking distance from where we lived. The had an open salad bar out in the dining area. We would go and stack up on packaged saltine crackers and containers of ranch dressing. We'd each grab hands full of condiments, croutons, and coffee creamer to drink. We qualified for free school lunch which was pretty much the same type of food provided at the food banks, so we weren't starved at all.

The resentment that I felt from my family gloating about the help they gave my mom fueled my independence. As a natural nurturer, I would do anything to make someone else smile or help someone out and I would never talk about it. The only way someone would hear of the help I provided to anyone was if they themselves told. In turn, it became hard for me to accept help from anyone out of fear that I'd appear needy. It became hard for me to trust anyone who shared with me their good deeds towards someone else. It's even harder for me to forgive anyone who speaks of anything they did for me.

CHAPTER 5.

My parents divorced by the time I was 7 years old. Although my dad had given up drugs and recommitted himself to God his flesh was weak. He struggled with resisting a different temptation. Another baby girl was conceived outside of the covenant of their marriage. He shared this child with a woman we all knew from the church, Sister Allison – God rest her soul. I just remember there was a big dispute about her wanting to name the baby Eugenia, after my father. My mother was outraged. Still, she didn't cuss. Sister Allison wasn't the only one. There was sister Sherry too.

Mama put daddy out of the house, and he went to live with Sister Delores. We knew her from the church. She was very active in ministry and could cook her behind off. We made fun of the way she'd shout. She'd run around the church speaking in tongues. It was always the same tongues which is what we found to be the funniest part. I naively believed that she was just doing her Christian duty by taking my daddy in after Mama put him out.

It was during one of our weekend visits with Daddy at Sister Delores' house that I'd lose a little more hope in the good of the world. The image of a holy woman of God with my daddy's naked body rubbing up against hers gave me a shock.

I must've startled my dad when I opened the wrong door looking for the bathroom in the middle of the night. "Who told you to come out of that room?" he shouted angrily.

He was mad at me. I was confused. She was naked. I was confused.

I was confused about a lot of things. Everything was going wrong. My eyes were beginning to open to just how sinful the world really was. I watched my dad have inappropriate intimate encounters with so many of his lady friends. Many of them members of the church. Daddy was a delivered from his addiction to chemical substances. He still had a weakness for the ladies.

I don't remember her name but there was one that I grew particularly fond of. She was pretty. We called her the hat lady. Not only did she wear big elegant hats on Sundays she made them herself. In her house she had a room with a sewing machine, fabric and a plethora of embellishments for her hats that she would create and sell them for profit. She always dressed in designer clothes and smelled of the sweetest perfumes. She smelled like cotton candy. She created and sold the biggest most extravagant hats; however, she wore more conservative hats. Nothing to bold or blinding to the people that sat behind her.

Even though she was dating my dad I admired her classiness. She was so stylish, tasteful and ambitious. She seemed to have all her stuff together. I respected her for the way she carried herself like a lady boss. She was strong, smart, and a determined entrepreneur. As her temporary stepdaughters she made sure that whenever we stepped out with her, we would mirror her level of class. We had to be neatly groomed and poised like princesses. I wondered how she ended up with my dad. Like all the others, that relationship didn't last very long. She was there one day and gone the next. I'd always hoped to one day see her again, but I wouldn't dare ask about her. I knew to stay in a child's place. Daddy had already moved on to another woman anyway.

My mom was pulling some attention of her own from some potential male suitors. She became close to the bus driver who was assigned to our route to school every morning. He had a daughter that went to the same school. That made it convenient to schedule play dates.

I don't remember my mom ever being without a man either. As the custodial parent we spent more time with her and only saw my dad every other weekend – if that. Every time she got a new man – which was often – we changed residents and had to quickly get acclimated to the new man's rules and disposition. The expectations changed with each guy and so would my mom. Those men could physically discipline us whenever we weren't in compliance with the new world order.

My mom never did get to finish nursing school. She was now a single mother raising 6 kids on her own. We were still on welfare and living off any other government assistance. The men she dated would be another source of income and ultimately her security net.

The earliest memory I have of meeting my stepmother was at Grandma Hinds funeral. She was pregnant with my brother Jonathan. She and my daddy had gotten married and he was now on baby #8. She already had a son, Hamish who was about my age at the time. We were mean to him, relentlessly teasing him because he had a heavy Jamaican accent.

The news of daddy getting married to another woman and finding out she was pregnant hit my mom hard. Shortly thereafter she'd find a love of her own. He stood about 5 ft 7 inches tall. Dark chocolate complexion with a jerry curl and a gold tooth. He was short but stocky. Very charismatic. Gold rings on every finger and Cuban link chains around his neck.

His pimp look matched his pimp car. It was a champagne colored old school Cadillac.

The first time we met the man that we'd come to call our "stepdad" he'd given my mom a ride to pick us up from school. He took us to Oswald Park; it was just up the street, but he came bearing gifts. A trunk full of cotton candy, chips, soda, lollypops, and all the snacks we'd see at the corner store but could never afford. He had the entire candy isle from the store in the trunk of his car. We were more than willing to sell off our own mama for this sugar buffet and a swing.

They never legally married but within a matter of weeks, we were moving in with him. We would now become a family of 8 in a two-bedroom apartment in South East Ft. Lauderdale. Everyone viewed him as this knight in shining armor having rescued a poor single mother and her six nappy headed kids from their low-income housing apartment in the hood without electricity or water. He helped her to get a job as a gas station attendant where he was the manager. She was finally happy and smiling all the time.

The only time there'd be trouble in paradise was when his friend Tommy came around. Tommy was a skinny white boy that hung around Allen like a lost puppy. He may have been in his early twenties standing about 5'8". Kind of dorky but he made us laugh. My mom hated him. She called him a stupid faggot. Her entire attitude would change anytime he came around it would upset her spirit. It was no secret that she despised the way he followed Allen around obeying his every command.

Becoming an instant family also meant Allen was able to discipline us. Nothing new about that. My mom had allowed the men she'd dated before to discipline us too. The rules changed every time my mom got a new man. His methods of discipline, however, were hard and barbaric. This was new. He beat us with a wooden paddle with holes like a tennis racquet. Whoever was getting paddled would have to be held down by the other siblings so they couldn't move. We'd go to school with our behinds bruised too badly too sit down. The holes from the paddle imprinted on our skin.

CHAPTER 6.

"A child's innocence is the one gift, that once stolen, can never be replaced."

— **Jaeda DeWalt**

My parents had both started new lives with their new loves and so began a new life for us.

The first time my stepfather touched me inappropriately I was 8 years old. He told my mom to keep me awake until he got home from his late-night shift at the gas station – so she did. I was getting in trouble for calling Dee a hoe. The massive pinch my mom gave my shoulder apparently wasn't punishment enough.

I was surprised when Dee ran to tell on me for calling her a hoe. I didn't even know what a hoe was. I just knew it was something mean.

I didn't tell on her for calling me a virgin, which was probably just as mean. I didn't know what that was either. I called her a hoe and she ran telling on me…like a hoe.

Midnight was approaching. He'd be getting off soon. I struggled to stay awake, but my mom did whatever he told her to do. She'd fallen asleep next to me on the couch, so I took advantage and closed my eyes as well.

I heard his keys turning in the lock. He was home. My heart began to beat so hard I could feel it in my eyes. My stomach was in knots. My first thought was to keep my eyes closed and pretend to still be asleep. Maybe he would feel some sympathy for me tonight and beat me in the morning. Then I remember he was crazy, and uncompromising. If he wanted to beat me, he was going to beat me no matter what. He might beat me and mama both for falling asleep after he specifically ordered her to keep me awake.

I tapped mama's leg to wake her up. She stood and walked over to the door to greet him.

As he entered, he didn't speak to me at all. Not verbally. He cut his eyes at me confirming that he was still very much upset for what I'd done. She shook his head with a side smirk expressing his disappointment and then proceeded to the shower.

My mom had gone to bed before he finished his shower. I sat frozen on the couch still struggling to stay awake. The fear of him waking me up with a slap or ice-cold water to my face or paddle to my behind was enough to keep me from dozing off too long. I could hear him turn off the shower. My heart was beating loudly again. There was the sound of drums beating throughout my entire body.

I raise my head cautiously to see him standing in the doorway of the bathroom wearing his navy-blue bathrobe with silken blue bordering. He didn't speak. He quietly walked past where I was sitting on the couch and took a seat at the bar outside the kitchen.

He turned the barstool beside him so that it no longer faced the bar, it now faced him. Tapping the floral cushion on the seat he summoned me to join him.

"Come over here" he ordered. His tone wasn't as angry as the look he'd given me before.

I quickly obeyed eager to end the torture of sleep deprivation and get this whooping already. He poured himself a glass of Crown Victoria as I climbed up on the stool.

"What's a hoe?" He asked as he took a sip from his glass. I swallowed hard but I'd rehearsed this in my head all night and he was way calmer than I'd expected him to be. I'd peeked into the dictionary at the definition of a hoe curious to know how much trouble I'd gotten m self into.

"A tool used for digging dirt." I responded. That's according to Webster, a hoe was just a tool used for digging. That was it. Nothing too bad. Maybe now that he knows what a hoe is, he'd let me go to bed with my behind unbruised.

I knew that wasn't the end of it by the way that he chuckled. "Nah Ima' show you what a hoe is." His tone was very matter of fact. He wasn't wasting any more time.

He placed his glass down on the counter and reach to touch my inner thigh that was visible underneath big the T-shirt I wore as pajamas.

"How does that feel."

I was frozen with fear. I wasn't sure how to respond. It felt weird but I couldn't tell him that. I was in shock. My brain couldn't even communicate to part my lips and form the words. I remained silent.

He moved his hand up further simultaneously lifting my shirt and spreading my legs. Now he was touching the seat of my panties.

"How does that feel now?" He asked again.

I wanted to say, it feels bad. It feels wrong. It feels weird. And if Mama would wake up and see this, she would kill you for touching me. I should scream and wake her up.

If you scream, I'll kill you. It's like he'd heard my thoughts out loud. I should stop thinking. I should just be quiet and do what he says so this can all be over, and I can go to bed.

"Close your eyes and keep them closed " He commanded.

I obeyed. Closing my eyes tightly as if this would somehow take me away from this dark place even for a moment.

He rolled my t-shirt all the way up to my waist exposing my entire body from the waist down. The moment he pulled my panties off was the moment I knew he was probably going to kill me and there was nothing I could do about it. He massaged the outside of my vagina and again asked me how it felt as if my response would eventually be something other than shock and fear. I tried hard not to cry. I felt a tear fall down the side of my face as he began to penetrate my vagina with his index finger. And this moment I wanted to die. He was using Vaseline as lubrication, but it hurt. I felt burning and ripping but was too scared to scream. My knees were moving closer together my hands clenched tightly to the sides the stool. I couldn't bear the pain. The tears were not flowing uncontrollably for my eyes still sealed with fear.

Finally, he stopped. "Get up and take your ass to bed." He whispered his command in my ear. The smell of alcohol BLANKING from his breath.

I leaped down from the chair and wiped my eyes. I felt a mix of feelings from confusion to fear and was apprehensive about what he might do next. "If you tell anyone I'll kill you and them too."

The next day Mama woke us up for school like any other day. I'd only gotten a few hours of sleep, but I didn't care if she was taking me to the worst of schools, I didn't want to be home alone with him.

I went through that day in a daze trying to pretend everything was normal. Wondering if I was crazy and dreamt it all up myself. I thought about telling Dee what happened, but I wasn't sure I could trust her. She was still mad at me from the day before. He'd warned me that he'd kill me and anybody I told about what he did. I won't tell anybody what happened, I decided. Nobody has to know. If he does it again, I'll tell - but he won't do it again because I will never call anybody else a hoe.

Some time went on and I started to feel some sense of normalcy. He only came home late at night when we were asleep. I figured all I had to do was be a good girl all the time and get into bed before he came home. That seemed like an easy fool proof plan and I'd never have to see him again. That dream was shattered when he decided to work the day shift and have Mama work nights. She went with it and of course this meant he'd be doing all the pickups, drop-offs, homework, dinner and most importantly our bedtime routine.

The first night of the New World Order he came into the bathroom as

I was taking a bath and locked the door. I felt the same Darkness come over me that I felt that night at the bar stools. He didn't say anything. Fear grew as I anticipated his next move. He took my Rag and created lather with the soap. I sat frozen and tried not to do anything to upset him as he bathed me like I was a toddler. I was almost nine years old. Fully capable of properly cleaning myself as I'd done since I was five. Almost every night I'd be the one giving my younger siblings their bath.

He washed my back and moved the bath rag around to wash my flat chest but stared hungrily as if they were fully grown breast. In a playful manner he pinched my nipple and laughed. Chicken Nuggets he called them. "Relax. I just wanted to make sure you were cleaning yourself the right way."

He lowered the rag down into the water.

As the lather escaped from the rag, with a gentle force he spread my legs apart and began stroking my vagina. My worst nightmare was happening all over again. This time he used two fingers to penetrate.

Once dressed I came out of the bathroom to find all my siblings laid out over the beds watching TV and eating candy and popcorn. It's as if I were in a Twilight Zone. Everyone was so happy. They probably didn't even notice how long I'd been in the tub. They had no idea of the hell that transpired in the next room.

He didn't make it a habit of joining me when I took a bath. He only did it if all the other five kids were distracted enough. I started taking my bath at earlier times to ensure that never happened. If I didn't feel safe, I just wouldn't take a bath at all. I change into my pajamas and when he asked if I had taken a bath, I'd say, yes.

But he was smarter than me. He knew what I was doing but instead of angering him it seemed to excite him. I was a game to him, a challenge perhaps; and he was determined to win. He did whatever he wanted to do. But he was calculated. So many times I'd successfully evading his bath time invasions, he became desperate other opportunities. If he wanted me and couldn't catch me during bath time, he just pulled me out of the bed when everyone was asleep. After a few months of penetrating me with his fingers and whatever kind of lubrication he could find around the house he started to rub my vagina with the head of his penis. It wouldn't go in at first, he'd massage it with lotion or oil and his fingers some more and try again. I hated it when he used his tongue and saliva. I would always think he could get me drunk through my vagina from all the alcohol he been drinking. He seemed to enjoy using his tongue. He would make moaning noises while biting on my clitoris and pulling all my Boba with his teeth. He would ask me if it felt good. It didn't, it hurt. I wasn't excited at all.

He started showing me more affection and attention than my siblings. I'd get nicer clothes and shoes. Mama wasn't allowed to hit me anymore, only him. Any time my mom would yell at me or threaten to whoop me if I didn't do one thing or another, he'd silence her. "You'd better not," he warned. If you hit her, I will hit you harder." She was afraid of him and after one or two times he never had to say it again.

CHAPTER 7.

I was awakened in the middle of the night by the thunderous sound of adults arguing. It had to be about 2 or 3 am.

"That nigga did it", my uncle was going off about something. He was always going off about something. This time was different though. He was emotionally upset. My mom got us up out of bed and got us dressed. We had no idea what was going on. We were barely awake. Something bad had happened.

My mom took us over to her friend, Sheila's house. I was too tired to eavesdrop, but Dee had managed to get all the tea and couldn't wait to spill it. My uncle had been arrested for sexual abuse against one of my cousins. All the ladies in the family were furious and wanted to kill him. I wondered if they'd support me the same. Somehow, I knew that now was not the right time to seek vengeance of my own. I'd only make things worse.

The family grew more divided after that. Emotions were running high with everyone picking sides and pointing blame. People were speaking with such negativity toward each other, cursing each other with their tongue. Even the children began to pick sides when hurtful words were spoken, and secrets were revealed.

Television was my gateway to all things unrealistic as far as I was concerned. My life was no fairytale, but I found comfort in the happy endings. They gave me hope. I found myself imagining I was Cinderella.

Allen being the evil stepmother and the stepsisters being my mom and my mischievous little sisters. I told myself I would never be weak like Cinderella though. I would be caring and kind, probably never feeling any sense of belonging in my world just like her. I wasn't going to wait for some fairy godmother or Prince Charming to come rescue me. I knew that was never going to happen. Not to someone like me, damaged and confused. I'd hoped that God would rescue me. The movie, "A Little Princess" taught me to be strong. I learned karate from watching the Karate Kid.

In 1993 Sister Act 2 was a convenient distraction from our everyday life. It was one of the rare occasions when we came together, my siblings and I, to sing dance and be merry. After watching the movie, a dozen times, we knew every song and every line to the movie. We'd get all dressed up to watch the movie in the living room. I related to several aspects of the movie, but the main character was Rita Watson who was played by who became and is still one of my favorite singers, Lauryn Hill. On the surface she appeared strong. She was often judged as angry and rebellious, but it was deeper than that. She had a song.

Although Rita had ambition, her life was not her own. She was not free to express herself.

Back at school, my fifth-grade teacher Miss Donaldson took notice to the fact that I'd never wanted to go home. I would find a reason to need to stay after school with her. We read, wrote and recited poetry together.

Miss Donaldson was an African American woman in her late 20s early 30s. She was fancy though. She wore long acrylic nails with designs on every finger and changed her hairstyle every two weeks. Her outfits always matched the color of her nail polish. She had a big booty and an even bigger attitude, but I loved her. She was my favorite teacher. Every week we had to memorize a new poem. It was through poetry that I learned to dream. My dreams would take me away from my nightmares.

"Well, son, I tell you: Life for me ain't been no crystal stair. It's had tacks in it, and splinters, and boards torn up, a place with no carpet on the floor – bare. But all the time I've been a 'climbin on and reachin' landins' and turnin' corners and sometimes goin' in the dark where there ain't been no light. So boy, don't you turn your back don't you sit down on these steps 'cause you find it's kinda' hard. Don't you fall now. For I'se still going honey. I'se still climbin'. And life for me ain't been no crystal stair." - Langston Hughes, Mother to Son

That was the year that we read the novel, "I Know Why the Caged Bird Sings" by Maya Angelou. She quickly became my favorite poet. I memorized every poem or short story written by Maya Angelou. I felt like I knew her in spirit. She understood me. I would often get lost in the writings of Nicki Geovanni and inspired by the powerful black women who used their voice. I'd lost my voice before I learned all the words I'd need to speak.

My plan was to be so smart I'd get double promoted and finish high school at age 15. Then I get a job at Checkers and move out. Nobody would have to know that anything ever happened. With my good grades and my short stories, I'd get scholarships to pay for me to go to college. I did enroll at Bethune-Cookman College, an HBCU, and become a writer. In school I won all the poetry and short story contest. I'd write for as long as I could even for the simplest of tasks. That made me happy. I became proficient with my words and was able to communicate and articulate on levels much higher than elementary school. Writing stories was how I escaped my reality.

She'd asked me if anyone was hitting me or touching me at home. She begged me to tell her the truth and promised me that I could trust her. I wanted to tell her the truth so badly, but I couldn't bring myself to do it. I thought about the consequences of me opening my mouth. My whole family would be embarrassed or dead and my mom would lose everything, and it would be all my fault. Maya Angelou didn't speak for five years after her opening her mouth resulted in deadly consequences for her mother's boyfriend. I wanted it to stop, but at what cost? Surely, I didn't want anyone to die. Thoughts and fears of what bad things might happen was enough to make remain silent and not say anything at all.

My mom was finally happy. Everyone was finally happy. We never went to bed hungry. We always had lights and running water. Nobody was talking about how poor my mama was and how much help she needed. I didn't want to be the cause of everyone else's misery. The only one suffering was me. As much as I hated my life, I was willing to sacrifice myself for my family to remain happy. We weren't poor anymore. I didn't think of it as a sacrifice at the time. I thought of it as one of those times the bible speaks about when God allows one person to go through pain and suffering so that others can be free.

Miss Donaldson must have voiced her concerns or said something to somebody because I hadn't. The next week my mom unexpectedly pulled us out of Rock Island Elementary and enrolled us at Croissant Park Elementary. She loved Rock Island and had relationships with all the teachers. They all knew our family well since my mom had so many kids, they had taught more than one of us. It was the middle of my fifth-grade year and I'd been enrolled there since Prekindergarten. She would never have withdrawn us unless he made her do it.

Croissant Park was a total culture shock. We left a school that was predominantly black kids and teachers where everybody looked like us. The teachers and kids at this school were different. There was no poetry club, they had chess and meteorology. The general population of students were white. The few black kids used proper grammar and words like, "cool" and "awesome" to express exclaim.

The only time African American history was mentioned or celebrated was during Black History Month in February. We read about Martin Luther King Jr and his dream, Rosa Parks ride in the bus, color pages about Malcolm X, and maybe a little something about how Harriet Tubman freed slaves. No mention of any of the other greats.

My first kiss was the best thing to happen to me at Croissant Park. His name was Thomas, but everyone called him T-Boy. His pickup line was, "Girl what your mama be feeding you, corn bread?" He wasn't the worst of boys, but he was a tough guy according to Croissant Park standards. If this were Rock Island he'd be getting teased for acting white, but here he was worshipped and celebrated for melanin. I appreciated his balance.

I wasn't allowed to have a boyfriend, but he kept asking so I agreed. He was the only black boy in my class and the closest thing I would ever get to familiarity. He was a shorty though. I didn't think he was very cute at all…but he was the only black boy in my class. Everyone expected us to be boyfriend and girlfriend for that very reason. We were both black, so we had to go together.

I didn't like the attention that came with having a boyfriend. Everyone whispered and giggled at us every time we'd be seen together. They discussed our business and watched every one of our interactions like soap opera.

Around the same time that I was adjusting to my new school, Dee was rebelling against the dictatorship in our home. She called the police on Allen one night when it was her turn to get a whooping. We all got a whooping that night, but Dee was 12 years old in 7th grade and had outgrown her willingness to obey. She was not about to let him beat us anymore and decided to do something about it. This would have been our way out. They'd take us away from there and put him in jail. He'd never be able to hurt us again. We could even get to live with Daddy.

The police did come, but it did not end the way she'd hoped. They ended up sharing laughs and shaking hands in a conversation with Allen exchanging stories about their parenting experiences with teenagers. His narcissistic nature, it was effortless for him to manipulate the officers portraying Dee as nothing but an ungrateful, disrespectful, spoiled little bratty preteen trying to escape his love taps of discipline. She was all that, but it was more than that. This was a legitimate case of abuse. Clearly the officers saw no need to further investigate beyond what Allen had provided as an explanation. The rest of us had already gotten out beatings. We stayed in the bedroom and listened as everything unfolded. Our behinds bruised and bloody from paddle. None us would dare come to her defense or side with her. We wanted none of what was about to happen after the officers left. We knew not to speak a word. We left Dee hanging out on a limb all alone.

The officer left and the next day Dee was out. Allen had given mom an ultimatum. Either she goes or I go. Dee had to go. It was in that moment that I knew she wouldn't ever protect us from him. She let him beat us and put her own daughter out at 12 years old. Where would she go?

Dee went to live with Daddy. Since he married his new wife, he was spending time with his kids, so we did not see him much. Mama had started her new life too. I was beginning to believe it when my mom said that since he couldn't be with her, he no longer cared about us. Not enough to fight for his right to see us. I wanted to go to Daddy's house too. I asked Mama if I could go, she picked up the phone and called Allen to tell him what I'd said. He came straight home and slapped my face. "I'm your daddy", he declared. Any time any of us would ask to visit Daddy he'd say those same three words in a very assertive tone silencing any continued protests and requests to visit him.

To make sure that his plan to isolate us from our father was working he'd test us to see if we were intimidated. He'd seem sincere in asking us "Y'all want to go see your daddy?", and if we said, "yes", he'd change his tone to a stronger one and remind us again, "I'm your daddy."

Whenever he'd ask in front of other people, we knew to say, no, or get a whoopin' when we got home. We got so good at pretending to hate to go see daddy. Gucci, my baby brother, was the third to the youngest of the six kids my parents shared. He began to believe the things Allen said about our father not wanting to see us and grew resentful. But I remembered how much daddy loved us. He was just scared of Allen. I'd heard him saying he'd kill my dad if he even came to his house. Daddy wasn't allowed to come to our house or call. Gucci didn't know that. I missed my daddy so much.

I waited until I was alone with my mom and pleaded with her, "Mama can I go stay with daddy too, please?" Mama picked up the phone. "Allen, Tiffany talking about she wanna go stay with Gene again." For some reason I thought that conversation would stay between us this time. At hope she'd seen the desperation in my face an felt some sympathy period or at least lead her to investigating my plea. If she just gave me a sign, let me know that she loved me or even cared enough to protect me. She was happy to see Allen upset with me. She hated that Allen seemed to favor me over the others – over her. Her power had shifted from her being my mother to her being my mammy as she hated me for it. She was happy to share the news of my request with Allen. She'd hoped that hearing this would infuriate him and somehow vindicate her. It did. He came home and whooped me good and she happily sat on my back pinning me down so that he could.

That night he punished me some more. He took me back to the gas station with him, he was back on the night shift. As it got later in the night, traffic dies down to about 1 to 2 cars per hour. He told me to go in the bathroom and take off my clothes. I knew what that meant. I complied. "I'm about to fuck the shit out of you."

He penetrated me violently on the floor of the gas station restroom. Underneath me was the cold floor contaminated with the urine, vomit common feces and other bodily fluids from The Dirty careless customers and the homeless community in the area. On top of me was what felt like 300 pounds of pig. He was sweating profusely as he exerted all his energy into every stroke and pound. I could feel the thick raindrops of sweat pouring from his body onto my face. My eyes were closed tightly my fists balled up by my side bracing for the beating of each stroke. I always closed my eyes. I didn't want to see. I didn't want to live.

CHAPTER 8.

"If I didn't define myself for myself, I will be crushed into other people's fantasies of me an eaten alive."

-Audre Lorde

I got to see Dee almost every day once I started middle school. She was an 8th grader and had her own group of friends as well as her own identity but she and her friends looked out for me unlike my older brother. He was in 7th grade but had already established a reputation for being a runner. He ran from every fright and would never stand up for himself. He wouldn't stand up for me. On the bus rides home, I'd have to defend myself against the boys trying to grab my butt. When I rejected them, they'd get upset and call me a bitch, shouting other obscenities.

"Are you just going to let them talk to her like that"? I overheard one of my brother's friends prompting him to stand up for me.

"She got it." He left me to defend myself. I lost respect for my older brother after that. He was tough and pushed around his sisters and his little brother at home but never had the courage to stand up against those boys. He wasn't a man. He never stood up to Allen, not once. Allen often belittled him and reminded him of his inferiority in the house. He'd get up in his face poking at him, pushing him both literally and figuratively daring him to blink. He never blinked.

Middle school was mystifying with all the different types of personalities. Some of my friends were scholars and excelled academically while others were involved in drugs and gang activity. I got along with both. My best friend in Middle school, Amy, tried to convince me to smoke cigarettes with her and some other kids after school. I thought about the D.A.R.E program and all it taught us about saying No to drugs and the book I'd read repeatedly, "Don't Say Yes When You Really Mean No". Peer pressure was not going to pressure me into killing myself. They laughed at me and called me scary for walking away, but I didn't care. I'd be offered other drugs countless times after that but was never felt tempted to try even once.

Everyone in middle school was "acting grown" and seemed to be determined to break all the rules or at least see how far they could bend them. I never felt pressure to break the rules along with everybody else because I was always afraid of the consequences. I knew the consequences of breaking the rules at school will be suspension, detention, or a juvenile detention center which was like jail for bad ass kids. I wanted no part of either one. The consequences are doing drugs according to the dare program was jail or death. I was a sergeant in the dare program in elementary school period what I learned gave me a fear of drugs so deep that I had the definition of a drug permanently embedded in my brain. *"A drug is anything other than food that causes a chemical change in your brain and bodily functions"*. Even chocolate and coffee were considered drugs because they had caffeine in them. I will boldly remind my friends that we are only 11 and 12 years old. We aren't old enough to drink beer or smoke cigarettes and it was illegal. Besides, drugs are bad. You could die the first time you try it. As corny as it sounds, I was never afraid of anyone being mad at me or of losing a friend behind me doing what I knew to be the right thing.

I would hang out with Dee and her friends as much as I could. It just felt safe. I knew that Dee saw me as her annoying little sister, but she never pushed me away or made me feel like I wasn't welcome. Her friends were just as inviting. They did bad things too, drinking and smoking, but they never tried to make me do it with them.

Dee had a boyfriend and her best friend was his cousin. They called her Pooh because she loved Winnie the Pooh. To them I was just Pooh's little sister. Tavares was Dee's boyfriend's cousin. He wanted to be my boyfriend, so they hooked us up. He was a year older than me and he went to a different school, but Dee would sneak and let me talk to him on the phone whenever she came over and we were home alone.

In the middle of my 6th grade year at Attucks Middle School we moved again from the 2-bedroom apartment into a house. Our new home was a house with a pool in the backyard. We had a back yard now.

Moving meant we'd have to change schools because Attucks was too far from where we lived. My first day heading to William Dandy Middle school on the school bus was just another reminder of the evil in the world.

I boarded the bus and sat down in the first available seat.

"No, she didn't. I know this bitch is not sitting in my seat." This girl was pissed off about somebody sitting in her seat. I looked around confirming that she was talking about me. "Get up now", she commanded. There was no assigned seating on the bus and the driver told me to sit anywhere. Besides, there was nowhere else for me to sit but on the floor. I didn't want any trouble, but I was not about to sit on the floor. I knew not to engage with these types of people especially since I was new to the school. I'd probably get jumped. Me ignoring her only invited her to become more dramatic. She was getting loud in her protest to sit alone on the bus. The bus driver refused to move the bus until she sat down so eventually, she did. The entire ride to school she ranted on. Her friends encouraging it and laughing. "If she sits in my seat tomorrow Ima beat her ass, I know that".

The next morning, I tried to find a different seat, but they were all taken. She sat closer to the isle to block me from taking a seat next to her.

"Excuse me." I tried to be polite, but I was obviously irritated.

"She aint talking to me." The girl folded her arms and sat in protest. She better sits her ass on the floor I don't care but she isn't sitting here."

"I'm not sitting on no floor." I advised.

"I can't move this bus until everyone is seated, young lady" The bus driver was ordering me to sit down but wasn't saying anything to make the girl move over. The bus echoed with the commands of other students for me to sit down as well. Did they expect me to push her over? They *wanted* us to fight.

"Y'all better leave her alone that's my cousin". A voice came from the front of the bus in my defense. "Girl move over and let her sit down. And if you touch her you gotta fight me." This girl was an 8th grader and not my cousin but I recognized her as one of Dee friends.

"Leave that girl alone and let her sit down." The bus driver suddenly decided to chime in. Finally, the girl moved her legs into the isle to allow me to sit down next to the window.

"You lucky you ain't stank." She continued to mumble and talk trash to her friends, but she feared my sister's friend, so she left me alone.

The kids at this school were constantly testing each other's toughness. There were kids from different neighborhoods that attended the school and they'd all formed their different cliques. There were several gangs that had formed based on where they lived or what hood they were from.

At home I was still dealing with my other predicament. My mom and Allen were rotating shifts now that they'd hired another attendant. Allen was offered a better paying position at a carpet cleaning warehouse and was transitioning to work their full time. On the occasion that he was the one at home with us at night I would be nervous. The chances of him pulling me out of bed were great.

When my mom came home early from her shift one night, he'd just finished sweating on top of me. She wasn't able to open the locked door to her own bedroom and began beating and kicking at the door instead shouting, "Open up this door. Open the door NOW!" My first reaction was to run into the closet and hide. I thought about opening the door unclothed so that everything would be revealed. Then I thought about how much ridicule my cousin had endured. We hadn't seen our cousins in over a year since that happened. Still… this could be my way out. I should take it. I crawled out of the closet and went to open the door. My mom had gone to try to find a hanger or something she could use to break in. Allen was sitting on the bed in his robe. His demeanor was calm. He seemed unbothered which left me confused.

Then in a whisper he uttered the words, "I'll kill you." I stepped away from the door and quickly put my pajamas back on before reaching up to open the door. Before I could turn the lock, the door flew open. My mom, with a hanger in her hand and rage in her eyes stormed in.

"What's going on? What are you doing inhere with the door locked?" She directed her line of questioning toward me instead of him.

I looked back at Allen expecting him to respond. With his eyebrows raised and a slight grin he remained silent and shrugged his shoulders leaving it up to me to decide. I was afraid both of him and of my mother. If I said the wrong thing, things could get bad fast. My mom was upset but she had shown me in previous situations that I was not exactly her favorite. I did not believe she would protect me. If she did, and tried to attack him for what he'd done, he could kill us both.

"I came in here to watch TV and fell asleep." I lied.

"Why was the door locked?" She was still shouting.

"I didn't know it was locked. I must've locked it by accident."

She lowered her tone in an uncanny retreat. "Take your ass to bed", she commanded. To my surprise that was the end of that. She'd accepted my poorly derived explanation for why I was in the room with the door locked. It was as if she knew exactly why I was in the room but didn't really want to confront the reality.

The next day was a Saturday. She was headed off to work leaving him at home with us again. She called me outside just after she'd started up the car to leave.

"I don't want you going in that room again, you hear me?"

"Yes ma'am."

"Keep your grown ass out of my room and away from my man." She offered her final warning just before pulling off. I stayed outside in a daze for a few moments just to gather my thoughts. Once I saw my mom clear the corner I headed back inside.

In the street, some boys I'd seen at school were joy riding in an SUV driving erratically. It was about 4 of them. They couldn't have been older than 12 or 13 years old and they were driving. It was on the news later that those boys had stolen that car. It was a miracle that no one was hurt. Everyone was raving about it at school.

William Dandy Middle school was just across the street from my first Elementary school. There were a lot of familiar faces that I'd recognized from elementary school. The faces were familiar but the people I once knew as friends, had changed.

I was in 5th grade when we withdrew from Rock Island and enrolled at Croissant Park. It was now the middle of 6th grade. Middle school was tough. A lot had changed over the year. My experiences would become life lessons stored in my long-term memory.

Substitute teachers were going home in tears or stretchers. The students were so disrespectful. The students felt empowered knowing they could push an adult to defeat. One student purposely left a partially smoked cigarette on the whiteboard. When the substitute asked who it did, no one would tell. The principal came in and threatened to suspend everyone in the class if someone didn't tell her who left the cigarette there. I thought I was doing the right thing when I raised my hand to tell. After class the students all surrounded me and the girl I'd told on. She wanted to fight. I didn't want any trouble, but I was ready to defend myself. As the crowd grew bigger it drew the attention of teachers whose classrooms were nearby. Once the students saw the teachers coming everyone scattered.

The girl began to taunt me for days after that. She'd intentionally bump into me as I walked the halls to go to class. She wanted me to react so that we could fight, and I'd get in trouble. In gym class I was playing double-dutch with my friends and she jumped into the rope as I was turning. It was my friend's turn to jump. My friend was afraid to speak up. I was tired of this girl and all the other bullies at the school. There were many.

I dropped the rope in protest and went to sit down in the bleachers. As expected, the girl was mad. She shouted curse words and threats from the court daring me to come down from the bleachers to fight. She wanted to fight me so badly but wouldn't come up 3 isles into the bleachers to get at me. She just wanted to look big and bad in front of her friends. I smiled unconsciously at the revelation almost daring her to come into the bleachers. I imagined pushing her down the stairs and breaking her neck.

One of the boys from the stolen car incident asked me to be his girlfriend. It was more of a command. He had chosen me to be his girlfriend. I wasn't allowed to have a boyfriend and I was already in a top-secret relationship with Dee's boyfriend's cousin. When I refused his advances, he promised to get his crew to beat up my brother. I did not warn my brother because I didn't take him seriously. It wasn't until that afternoon as we were walking home after school. We were almost halfway home when a crowd came running across the 4-lane highway. We could hear them chanting their war song behind us and we knew it meant they were looking to attack someone. We continued walking, but more quickly, until they had us surrounded. Three of the boys held me back as the others jumped my brother. I was screaming for him to run home. As soon as he was able to escape the mob he did. They didn't run after him and he never looked back to make sure I was safe. He just kept running.

The boys released me without harm. "I told you we were gonna get him." The boy boasted with a smile feeling vindicated after his rejection. When my brother came home all bloody and bruised my parents went out to the school. The school couldn't do anything because it happened off campus. Neither of us were willing to give names to the police. We didn't trust them to protect us from the backlash.

Seventh grade was only a bit easier. Students were still fighting, gangbanging, and having sex underneath the portables. I'd tested high enough on the 6th grade state exams to be placed into the Magnet Program with the smart kids. The school kept the magnet students separate from general education and the instance of crime was far less. The classroom disruptions were minimal as we read Chronicles of Narnia, The Lion the Witch and The Wardrobe.

The Magnet kids committed crimes of a different sort. They'd prank each other and tell corny "yo mama" jokes. Dramatic sneezes, dropping pencils and then purposely falling out of their chair to retrieve it was their way to disrupt the class. One student told me to smell his finger and I did. In the middle of the thunderous laughter he confessed that he'd just been scratching his testicles. I didn't tell on him, but someone did. The teacher pulled me aside after class and asked me if it were true what had happened. I told her that it was. She hugged me and made me promise to never allow someone to do something so disgusting and disrespectful to me. She made me promise to always speak up and tell whenever someone does anything that makes me feel in the least bit uncomfortable. The last time I told on someone I almost got jumped by a mob of general ed students. The teachers in the magnet program were more protective and seemed to care more about our safety. She saw to it that the boy was suspended for 3 days for his prank.

I earned my 1st F on my report card that year. It was in Algebra 1. The Algebra 1 teacher was mean. Being transferred into her class from regular 6th grade mathematics and without pre-algebra I was confused about the problems and formulas I had to solve. I didn't understand the vocabulary and she didn't have the patience to explain it to me. I remember getting a zero for the day because I sneezed too loudly. Surprisingly, my parents weren't upset about the F. They never even acknowledged it. I, however, was disappointed in myself. I felt like a failure and decided that I would never be good at Algebra so why even try. The next year I passed Algebra 1 with a C.

Tavares, the cousin that Dee and her boyfriend had set me up with transferred to this school. So was my friend, Amy. Amy was no longer interested in being my friend. She had joined a gang and that was her family now. She was in general ed so we would only see each other in passing or after school. Tavares was rarely in school. He was always suspended for fighting but whenever he was on campus, he'd meet me in between classes and walk me to class. He was involved in gang activities as well, but I wasn't afraid. He was protective of me and encouraged me to keep being a good girl.

My brother and I had started taking a different route home since he got jumped by those boys. Our new route encompassed walking in the opposite direction away from our home to the bus stop and catching the city bus home. My parents felt that this route would keep my brother safe as the boys lived in our neighborhood and would be looking for him to walk that way.

This new route brought safety to my brother but brought me face to face with my old friend, Amy and her crew. We were no longer friends but before that day I didn't view her as an enemy. We were standing at the bus stop in front of her apartment complex when she approached me with her friends close behind.

"I heard you were talking about me…" That was code for *I want to fight you, but I don't have a reason or the balls to just hit you*. Her crew surrounded us, and I knew how this was going to play out. She and I would start fighting so that she could look tough in front of her friends if she beat me up. If her friends saw that I was getting the best of her, they would jump in and help her beat me up. I think I was more annoyed at her cowardly approach. We'd been best friends and shared secrets. She cried to me when her boyfriend broke up with her. Now, she was leading these goons in setting me up to get jumped and she chose "*I heard you were talking about me*" as her punch line (pun intended). I was hurt and furious but never afraid. I knew she wasn't bad. She hung out with bad girls for whatever reason, but she wasn't bad.

My anger and irritation were prevalent in my tone. "Amy if I was talking about you, you know damn well you wouldn't have to hear it from anyone else." I walked closer to her so that we were standing nose to nose. "If you want to fight me then hit me but don't let your friends boost you up to get knocked down," I had now become the aggressor, ready for whatever happened next. I remember her repeating, "You better put your hands down" stalling as she tried to build up the courage to hit me and set off the brawl. The crowd had gotten big along the road by the bus stop. A car pulled up on the side of the street with high school students inside. The city bus pulled up behind the car blowing the horn for them to move. The crowd started to disburse. Amy's friends pulled her back in their retreat, she was getting louder and more reckless with her trash talk now that she was being held back.

"What y'all doing?" The high school students exited the car. They weren't coming to break up the fight they were looking for entertainment. They wanted to see what was happening. From the car I heard a voice say, "That's Pooh's sister."

"That's Pooh's sister? Which one?" Even though Dee was in high school her affiliation through her boyfriend was our refuge that day. Her friends gave us a ride home to make sure we stayed safe. After that we were reassigned to the school bus.

CHAPTER 9.

"The most common way people give up their power is by thinking they don't have any."

— **Alice Walker**

I always knew this day would come. The moment I saw it, I felt both scared and relieved. Excited but apprehensive. Excited that I was becoming a woman. Soon enough I'd be able to have children of my own. I'd love them and protect them and live for them in all the ways my mom neglected to. I was apprehensive about knowing all the rules of becoming a woman. I always dreamed of becoming a mother and a wife, but I understood that these roles came with responsibilities. Responsibilities that a 13-year-old girl was not prepared to take on. Relieved because maybe now Allen wouldn't hurt me anymore now that I can get pregnant. Scared that maybe he still will.

I told mama first, knowing she'd go tell Allen. I slept good at night knowing he wouldn't be coming into my room. It was the best sleep I've had in years. That dream was abruptly interrupted. After 7 days had passed, he didn't even ask if my period was done. I had to work the night shift at the station.

My apprehension gave me the courage to politely ask him to stop this.

Getting him upset was a risk I was willing to take but if I could just reason with him perhaps, he would show mercy. I pleaded with him reminding him that I could get pregnant now. He wasn't moved. He didn't acknowledge my plea nor my tears at all. He commanded me to go into the bathroom and get undressed.

He wasn't ever going to let me go. "I'm going to be his prisoner and live in this hell until the day I move out." I thought. He was on top of me again. Heavy, smelling like alcohol, sweat dripping from his body onto my face. I just cried silently as I always did. And that moment I just felt so hopeless in a long period no one sees my tears. No one hears my cries. No one even cares. My biggest fear at this point had become getting pregnant. If I was to become pregnant by my stepfather, I'd end my life without a second thought.

When he was done, he laid on top of me. I could barely breathe. And that moment I *wanted* to stop breathing and end my existence. I contemplated suicide many more times since that day I just couldn't think of a way to end my life suffering without hurting myself. I wanted it to be over quickly and painlessly.

One day I had an idea that I could kill HIM instead. I could end his life and my torture at the same time. He has a life insurance policy so mama wouldn't have to lose the house and we wouldn't have to move back to the hood. Everyone could still be happy. I'd make it look like an accident. I could hit him over the head with a pot and push him into the pool, so he'd drown, and it would look like an accidental drowning. I chuckled to myself at the thought. This man weighs like 5,000 pounds compared to me, a petite 13-year-old girl. Still, I was willing to try. I'd been watching enough murders on much Lifetime Television murders, this could work.

I lured him out by the pool by telling him that something was stuck in the pool pump. There was a wooden barrier built around the pool pump. To access the pump, we needed to lift the door vertically from the base. When he leaned over to check it out, I dropped the heavy wooden door covering the pool pump onto his head.

Big mistake. He didn't die. All that did was make him mad. He turned around and gave me this death stare but resisted the urge to hit me. It looked like he was more focused on the pain and trying not to scream out in pain.

"I'm sorry." I fearfully proclaimed.

"Hold the goddamn door, man" he commanded in a tone as scary as the death stare, he'd given me. Fortunately, he'd never suspected it was an attempt to end his life. He thought I'd accidently dropped the door on his head being clumsy or distracted. I won't get a second attempt. I gave up that plan and tried to think of a new one. It was probably wiser to just give it up but in my desperation for an absolution I just couldn't see how.

I could hear my little sisters screams coming from another room. She was getting a beating with the paddle for wetting the bed again. My little sister was bad as hell. She would steal candy and snacks from the kitchen then joined forces with my baby sister to blame it on me. My mom would believe them. Surely, they weren't BOTH lying on me. I couldn't ever convince her that they were. Sweetie, my baby sister and the knee baby, Faye, were closer to my mom than I was. They manipulated her just as much as she influenced them. Their resentment for me was rooted in my mom's hatred. They believed I was the favored one and stopped at nothing to see me lose favor with Allen. He was hurting me. They didn't know. I couldn't tell them.

This time she was getting what I thought was a much-deserved beating. She'd pushed me over into her wet spot several time before and I took her beating for wetting the bed. Witnessing this ass whoopin' felt like sweet vengeance. And the BONUS…Allen was ignoring me. He was distracted by how angry he was at her. Though it was only a temporary distraction, I welcomed these moments.

Later that afternoon Allen decided to let the rest of us go outside and ride our skates.

"OUTSIDE!!! Hell yeah!!" He rarely every let us go outside unless it was company over or a holiday party at our house. Within minutes we changed into our skates and play clothes and raced outside. It felt great to be a kid. I usually either had to steal a moment like this or feared that moments like this meant something bad was coming. Something was coming. I was outside enjoying life on this rare occasion talking with our neighbors across the street the Habersham's. Mr. Habersham drove a Cadillac with "Caddy Daddy" on the license plate. He was a garbage man and his wife were a teacher. They had 4 girls, Tabitha, Tamika, Terrika, and Tashana. Mr. Habersham was the only man in the house, but he seemed to enjoy it. The oldest daughter, Tabitha, was in high school and pregnant with her 1st child. This was not uncommon to our community at all and the family could not have been more supportive and loving. Terrika and I were closest in age and in the same grade. We became very close friends telling each other our deepest darkest secrets – except one. I wouldn't dare ever tell her my real deepest darkest secret.

I envied the Habersham family. It was like watching pure love. The love and unity shared between Mr. and Mrs. Habersham contributed to the closeness between the girls. I skated home and ran back into the house to get something I wanted to show Terrika. I enter through the back door by the pool straight into the kitchen. As I turned the corner into the dining room still geeked about all the fun I was having, I see my little sister seated on Allen's lap. His legs were open, and he was wearing his blue rope with nothing underneath. She quickly jumped down from his lap and sat in front of the TV in the family room. That entire scene looked very familiar only no one stumbled in and foiled his plans for me. I was frozen still. This seemed to be my body's natural reaction to shock or discomfort.

I felt a tremendous amount of guilt. I was so excited to get to go outside I didn't think about my little sister being punished by staying inside along with him while everyone gets to go outside. How closely that entire scene resembled my introduction to this hell of a life. I wanted to cry for her period I wanted to hug her period she was only 8 years old the same age that I was when he first targeted me. Now it was her?!

I'd convinced myself that it would all be over once I left for college, but I should have known better period I should have known he'd had another plan. No one was safe. I can't leave her alone with him. I had to protect her. Afterall there was still my baby sister Sweetie. I had to do something to stop him. Now he *must* die. I'd done very little to stand up for myself throughout all of this. Even though my sisters had been very difficult and mean to me I wanted to save her. I knew that they would not have behaved that way had they known the truth. I had already forgiven them in my heart.

I should have put an end to this sooner, there were so many opportunities, but I was afraid. Instead of going back outside I pretended I wanted to watch TV too. I went inside on the couch next to where Faye sat on the floor. I was never bold and brave enough to stand up for myself against him but seeing my little sister being targeted and headed towards years of the same dramatic experience gave me the courage to want to defend her in whatever way a 13-year-old girl could.

That night when it was time for bed, we went to bed together. I slept in the bed next to her so that I would feel her every move. He did come into our room that night, but it wasn't for her period he snatched me from my bed and beat me for not washing the dishes before going to bed. Faye was safely sleeping in bed; I went to do the dishes. Allen had fallen asleep on the couch by the time I was done.

He was laid out on his back on the couch sleeping with his mouth open. His snores loud and rumbling like a freight train. I had a large kitchen knife in my hand and the fully exposed neck of a piece of shit sleeping on the couch. I stood over him with the knife held high up in the air above his head. All I had to do was lower my arms with the strength of every ounce of anger, hate, rage, resentment. For every day of my life that he took away from me.

I couldn't.

I couldn't bring myself to do it.

Disappointed in myself for being so weak I slowly lowered the knife from the air and placed it on the sofa next to his head. I dragged myself to bed.

The next morning, he woke everyone up and lined the 5 of us upside by side threatening to beat all of us one by one if we didn't say who left the knife beside his head. I no longer cared about dying. 'It was me", I confessed in all hopelessness. "I was cleaning the knife in the kitchen when I came to watch a commercial on the TV. I must've put it down and forgotten about it."

He knew that wasn't the truth. I showed no emotion, no Fear. With my confession I looked straight into his eyes and didn't blink once. He saw the rage in my eyes, and he knew.

His opportunity for vengeance came shortly thereafter. Dee, who was now 16 and pregnant with her first child, had spotted my necklace around Tavares's neck and shared this information with my mom. It was a gold necklace personalized with my name. Very distinctive. I'd let him wear it when we were at school, after school one day he was on his way to meet me at my bus when he got into a fight and was suspended again. I never got it back. My mom, of course, couldn't wait to share this information with Allen. She still wasn't allowed to physically discipline me although I don't think she ever really wanted to. She wasn't the disciplinarian for any of us anymore. He distributed the paddling, but I think it gave her more joy to see him do it.

When Allen arrived home, he asked me to bring him my necklace. I told him that I'd lost it which wasn't entirely false. I'd assumed that it was broken, damaged, or lost sometime during or after the fight. I wasn't expecting the he'd still have it but apparently, he did, and he was wearing it proudly. Allen grabbed me by my hair and threw me into the car.

He made me show him where the boy lived and knock on the door. I was in tears as I knocked on the door hoping no one was home. This was embarrassing. Tavares came to the door with his older brother and his Rastafarian stepfather. Allen aggressively demanded the necklace back from Tavares and warned him to stay away from me. He reluctantly complied under the advice of his stepfather who'd advised him to be peaceful.

"Now I'm about to take her home and beat her ass." Allen wasn't done humiliating me, he wanted to embarrass me so badly that I would never speak to Tavares again. He also wanted to intimidate Tavares so that he wouldn't speak to me. His attempt was only partially successful. He succeeded in embarrassing me, but he stopped nothing. After we left, Tavares rounded up his crew. They came to my street and circulated on their bikes outside the front of my house. They were chanting their war song and shouting obscenities from the street. Allen made us go into our rooms, but we watched from the window. He set himself up outside in the driveway on one of the lawn chairs in a standoff with the boys. They never trespassed pass the gate onto our property. They knew they weren't breaking any laws if they maintained their position in the street. They would be protected under the law only if they had a reason to believe someone was being harmed inside. There was no bloodshed that night. I slept peacefully knowing that even after the crowd disbursed, they were still patrolling the street into the night in my defense.

CHAPTER 10

He had been my boyfriend for about a year and we'd never even kissed. We only saw each other at school but he was always suspended so even that was rare. He was well on his way to be a high school drop-out. Maybe even on his way to prison. Maybe both. But this good girl was ready to show her bad boy that she could be bad too. In a letter to him I let him know just that.

"We've been going together for a year now and I'm ready to show you what I can do. I know you probably think I'm scared, or you might hurt me but it's me that might hurt you. My stepdad is working early on Friday. Me and Tanesha are going to skip school and come to your house. I want you to make love to me. I love you."

I placed the letter in my underwear drawer for safe keeping until I can get it to him, but I never got the chance. He was never at school. Always hanging around in the streets – the one place I'd never be. Eventually I'd forgotten I'd written the letter to him at all.

Sometime later I was catching the bus to work after school. Everything felt normal. I had no reason to suspect the night would end with me in a hospital. I arrived at the warehouse, took some calls, and scheduled some cleanings as I normally would. Around 5:00 I said goodnight to the ladies in the sewing room and started cleaning. For the next couple of hours, the cleaning vans came in one by one as the workers finished up their routes. The drivers would turn in their keys and get into their personal vehicles to go home.

After I'd cleaned every desk, dumped every garbage, and vacuumed the second-floor office spaces, I went down to the first floor to clean. I don't recall seeing Allen at all the entire time. It was almost time for us to go home when he entered where I was cleaning up in the sewing room. He looked angry…very angry.

"You are fucking now?" He asked as if he had already concluded that I was. I wasn't.

"No."

"Stop lying. I read you fucking letter to your little boyfriend. You got a boyfriend?" There was an eerie glare of darkness in his eyes. Almost evil. He was sweating profusely and breathing hard which wasn't necessarily uncommon, but it looked like he'd been doing some physical work.

"I'm not lying. I don't have a boyfriend." I tried to sound convincing. He was scaring me. I had never seen him this angry before. I lied about not having a boyfriend, but I knew that right now would not have been a good time to disclose that information. I didn't remember what all I'd written in the letter, but I knew that Allen had read it. Whatever was written had him beyond pissed off with me. He had this look of rage in his eyes that said, *"you're going to die tonight."*

"Take your clothes off and lay down on the table." He commanded. There was no way I was about to take my clothes off and lay down on the table. I didn't know what would happen next. I remember how he'd violently raped me before when I asked to see my dad. That time it was ego, pride and some jealousy but this time it was rage.

"No." I shook my head and backed away as I refused. He had gotten uncomfortably close. He was now on the opposite side of the sewing table where I stood. He took a couple of deep breaths before he leapt over the table to grab me. I wasn't fast enough. He was able to grab my braids. Two of my braids were torn from my scalp leaving square shaped bald spots along my hairline as I put up a fight trying to get away. If he wasn't ready to kill me before, he'd surely do it now that I've rejected him and put up a fight. I felt him trying to get his arm around my neck. I couldn't let that happen. I kicked and screamed and did everything I could to prevent him from getting a handle on any part of my body. He still had me by my hair which occupied one of his hands, but I kept wriggling as hard and as fast as I could. Somehow, I was able to free myself from his grip and charged out of the back door of the warehouse.

I ran away as fast as I could. I could hear his heavy footsteps as he followed close behind me, but I never looked back. I just kept running. It had gotten dark outside. People were already in their homes preparing their families for the next day. Where would I go? How would I get back home? I couldn't go back to him. It was time to end this. I spotted an office building nearby with the light still on. I no longer heard Allen's footsteps behind me. Maybe he'd turned back to get the car. I advanced toward the light.

Once I arrived, I knocked on the door with desperation. Praying that someone would let me in. Finally, a man opened the door and I begged him to let me in.

"Please let me in there's somebody chasing me he's right behind me, please!!" The man let me in.

"Who's chasing you?" He asked. There was another man on the inside. Skinny little white me. He'd tear them apart. The single second of relief that I felt was interrupted when the second man went outside to investigate who might be following me.

"No no no! Don't go outside, PLEASE." I screamed. "He will kill all of us." I remember thinking how stupid this man was to go outside. He must be crazy. Was he *TRYING* to get killed? "He's been to jail before and he isn't afraid to go back." I warned.

The man hurried back inside to join his friend who was trying to console me. "I don't see anyone." My face, covered in tears, was buried into this stranger's stomach as if I'd known him all my life. I was ready for this to be over. Something about him made me feel safe. Through my tears and all my emotions, I told him everything. I told him how my stepdad had been sexually abusing me since I was 8 years old. How he threatened to hurt me and my family if I ever told anyone. How he'd tried to hurt me that night just before I ran away from him. The other man was on the phone with the police telling them everything I said.

"I need to call my mom" I requested. I couldn't wait to hear her voice and I knew she couldn't wait to hear mine. I thought she must be worried sick. Surely, she'd be relieved to know that I was okay. They allowed me to use the phone to call my mom, but the conversation didn't go as I thought it would.

"Mommy."

"Tiffany, where are you." She sounds angry.

"Mommy I need you to come gets me, please."

"I'm not coming to get you. You better get back to that warehouse and come home with Allen."

"Mommy I don't want to go back there because…" She wouldn't let me speak. She started screaming at me to go back, NOW! "When that car pulls up in the yard you better be in it." She wouldn't listen me.

Allen had already gotten to her apparently. She accused me of running away from home because of the letter which lead me to believe that was what he'd told her. She was shouting at the top of her lungs. Her yelling echoed in my ear through the phone until I hung up. She wasn't going to listen to me. She wasn't going to protect me. I felt hopelessness and alone and I hung up the phone. I never raised my head to look into the eyes of the two men who stood in shock at what had just transpired.

Shortly thereafter there was a knock at the door. It was the police. The two men went to the door and a female officer came inside. She reached out her hands to me with a semi smile and I stood to go to her. This would be the first time I'd breathe a sigh of relief. As we stood in the doorway, she pointed toward one of the patrol cars and asked, "Is that him?"

Allen sat in the back of the patrol car; his hands cuffed behind his back. I nodded to let the officer know that was indeed the man I was running away from. He shook his head and then looked down. At the time I thought it was a look of disappointment. I'd later learn that he was denying that he'd done anything wrong at all. The officer placed her arms on my shoulders and escorted me to another patrol car. Our next stop would be the hospital.

The signage read "Sexual Assault Treatment Center". There were more officers there. They asked me to tell them everything that had happened. I did. I told them everything from the beginning. They asked specific questions like, when was the date of last time he'd penetrated me. I remembered it well because it was two days ago. They carefully noted my usage of words and how I described my body. They asked if he had ever asked me to perform oral sex acts or penetrated me anally. I told them he had.

After the police finished asking their questions, I was taken into another room with an examination table. The room was cold and intimidating with a big white light shining directly on the table. I had no idea what was about to happen. Someone with a clipboard, wearing scrubs and gloves came in. She handed me a hospital gown and told me to take off my clothes and lay down on the table. I looked to the lady officer who was still there beside me. She gave me another slight smile and nodded to let me know it was okay. I trusted her.

The doctor began an invasive procedure examining my vagina with a cotton swab. She inserted several things into my vagina that night, even taking pictures and combing my pubic hairs onto a petri dish. It was over relatively quickly but I could never relax.

When that was over, the officer walked me over to the reception area where my mom waited with my uncle Brannon. This time I felt the hug I'd been waiting for.

"I'm so sorry, baby." She said as she held me tight. She was crying. I cried tears of relief. It was over.

TIFFANY YOUNG

CHAPTER 11

I was alone inside an empty room that appeared to be my room inside my home. It looked the same, but no one was home except me. It was dark outside from the overcast created by the storm clouds. The sky was rumbling with warning signs of something malevolent. I saw the funnel forming in the clouds and immediately felt fear growing inside my chest. I ran to warn my family but still I couldn't find anyone. This was my house but where is everyone? It was eerily quiet. I was all alone.

The tornado touched down howling. The core had to be about a mile wide. I had nowhere to go as it appeared to be coming straight toward my house. I ran and grabbed the mattress from the twin sized bunk bed in the boys' room and used that to cover myself in the bathtub. Our bathroom was in the center of the house. I'd remembered from being the meteorologists on the morning announcements at Croissant park that it was best to go to the most centralized location of the house away from any windows. The tornado was getting louder and closer. I closed the bathroom door and covered my entire body inside the tub. The tornado was ripping the walls off our house brick by brick. It tore off the roof. It's like it was coming for me. I wanted to see it.

I peeked out from underneath the mattress and saw that the tornado hovering above my head, but I wasn't afraid. I felt a sense of peace. It was a beautiful disaster just like me. It had destroyed my entire home except for the room that I was in leaving the bathroom untouched. I felt an uncanny connection to the storm. I closed my eyes and exhaled as I prepared to be lifted into the heavens along with the remanence of what was once my home. And then silence… it was gone.

It was my mother's voice that woke me from the dream. She was on the phone speaking to someone about what had happened the night before. Her tone had changed from that of a mother concerned with wanting to provide emotional support for her daughter who had experienced trauma. She was advocating for him. She expressed that she believed I'd been having sex with my boyfriend and was blaming it on her man to hurt her. I wasn't surprised. My life was becoming a real-life storm. I was at the center of all the noise awaiting an absolution that would never come.

She heard me getting dressed for school and opened my bedroom door. "Lay your ass back down, you ain't going nowhere". After giving her orders she closed the door without waiting to see if I complied. I didn't lay back down. I was confused. I wasn't allowed to come out of the room at all that day. Not even for food. I could hear people coming and going from the house, but no one came inside to check on me. It was as if no one knew I was there.

For about a month I was not allowed any contact with the outside world. I was restricted to my room whenever anyone came over. The news had been reporting on my stepfather's arrest. There was even an article in the paper. The journalists did name me in their reporting, but they did name him. They had included information that was indirectly exposing of my identity. Instead of our full address, they said we lived at the 1500 block of NW 12th street. Their poor attempts to shield the identity of the minor involved brought unwanted attention to my family. Word had traveled quickly that the girl in the story was me. As expected, people started speculating, deriving their own conclusions about the facts and picking sides.

The one time she did allow me to come out of my room and speak to someone they were members of his family coming to interrogate me. They needed to hear it for themselves and asked me to tell my "story". When I did, they called me a liar to my face and rebuked the demon inside of me.

She tried other approaches to get me to say I lied. Coercing me with legal terms I didn't understand. "You don't have to go through this, Tiffany. This can all go away, and nobody will be mad at you if you say it didn't happen. You can recant your story. Say it didn't happen. Tell them you made a mistake. They will let Alan out and we can get our old life back." I lowered my head as I considered her proposal. I *did* want this to all go away. He now knew not to mess with me anymore, but what about Angel and Tootie. He would kick me out and they would be defenseless against him. I couldn't lie for him. I couldn't bring myself even to lie for her. Finally, my mom advised that I would be attending a different school from now on. I loved my school and did not want to change but felt my exclaim of opposition would only make the situation worse.

My new school was most uncomfortable because Allen's nieces attended school there. In the first few days things were normal. Some of the students nicknamed me Dillard because I proudly wore the jacket from the rival school.

I'd recognized only a few faces from elementary and middle school, but these were not my friends. I didn't belong here. I hid in the linen closet underneath some clothes to avoid going to school. Dee and my mom search the house for all about 15 minutes looking for me. I thought I'd been caught when the doors to the linen closet opened. Whoever it was didn't see me under the bed comforters and closed the doors. After they couldn't find me, they concluded that I'd run away from home.

"I hope she stay gone." I heard my mom confess. "She said he penetrated her behind, but the report indicated that her butthole hadn't been touched." When the detectives asked me if he'd penetrated my butt I said, yes because I wasn't sure if "*doing it from behind*" was the same as "*doing it in my butt*". Nonetheless if the examination report showed all of that then it had to reveal other things that proved my story to be truthful otherwise. I was confused about what anal sex was, but the tests were performed to either support me or exonerated him. Surely, they'd found other stuff, but she chose to focus on that moment of confusion. She *wanted* to believe him. That's when I decided to run away for real. I waited in the closet until everyone was gone before I made my escape. In my mom's room were a dozen candles. She'd visited a medium and performed a truth séance to make me tell the truth about what happened.

Her instructions were written on a torn piece of lined yellow paper.

"Make her tell the truth," was written several times. She was to repeat this in her prayers with the Jesus candles and incense. I believed she'd put a spell on me. She didn't believe me and sought extreme measures to get me to tell the truth. Unbeknownst to her, should these antics be successful she was not going to get the results she sought. She'd only be sealing the fate of a pedophile and rapist.

I collected the piece of paper and some pocket change from the dresser before going into the kitchen to pack some snacks. I walked out of the house with no idea of where I'd go. I walked the streets of my neighborhood for hours avoiding the main streets or any street my mom would commonly travel. She wasn't looking for me and I surely didn't want to see her either. When school let out, I approached on of my friends and told her my mom had put me out. She invited me to come home with her. Her mom allowed me to sleep there under the impression that my mom had put me out. She didn't know I'd run away. I was only there a few days when she found out I wasn't being forthcoming. She ordered me to call home and let me mom know where I was. I didn't call my mom; however, I called my grandmother.

Our estranged relationship with our extended family made it difficult to trust any of them even a little but my grandmother had knowledge of what was going on. She knew I'd run away and that my mom was mistreating me. She invited me to come live with her until the court proceedings were done. Even though she offered a place of refuge, in the back of her mind she believed I was troubled. She'd perceived me to be promiscuous and dishonest. I'd only jumped out of one fire into a smaller one. If ever she couldn't find her money and any other item around the house right away, she accused me of stealing it. I'd hear her on the phone telling anyone who's listen about how I stole from her. She called and screamed threats and obscenities to my one of my good friends who was in the hospital having a baby. My grandmother couldn't find her lingerie and jumped to the conclusion that I'd stolen it and given it to my pregnant friend as a gift. My friend denied having seen the article of clothing, but my grandmother continued. She told her that she was sending the police to search her house. This left my friend in tears. Her grandmother was upset when she saw me later that day. She told me that I needed to return whatever I stole from my grandmother and leave her granddaughter out of my mess. I swore to her I had no idea what my grandmother was talking about but still she asked me to leave. When I went back home, I was angry with my grandmother. She was wearing the same piece of lingerie that she's accused me of stealing, which means she'd found it, but never called my friend to apologize. This tarnished my reputation with my friend's grandmother who'd always welcomed me into her home before this. This was not the only time my grandmother had accused me of stealing from her. She'd even suspected me of having sex with boys inside her house while she was at work. Neither of these were true. I never stole anything from her, and I never had any boys in her house while she was at work. I was braiding hair on the balcony to make some pocket change, but my clients were always girls. They were classmates from school or relatives of my friends – never boys.

At school, I missed the bus that was going to take me to my grandmother's house after school. The security officer offered to take me home. I trusted him enough to accept his offer. "I just need to drop something off at home first." He said.

We arrived at his house and he parked the car in his driveway before proceeding to go inside. I stayed inside the car. He insisted that I come inside, said it will be quick. Once inside he started to show me around his house. I stayed close to the front door under the belief that we were only there for him to grab something. We would be leaving right away. I complimented him on having a beautiful home.

"You like it?" He asked. He'd placed his keys on the counter and was coming toward me. I turned to face the door so that we could exit. As I reached for the doorknob, he placed his hand over mine and pulled my hand away from the door handle. "This can be your house if you want."

He turned my body around so that I was now facing him. He placed my hands around his waist and kneeled for a hug. His hands sunk down pass my lower back until they were on my backside. He firmly squeezed my butt with his hands and kissed my neck with his lips. This was our school resource officer. He was in a position of authority and power and sworn to serve and protect. I'd trusted that he was one the good guys. Here he was, in his early to mid to late 30's groping me, 15-year-old student, with an expectation of sex. I couldn't believe this was happening to me again. WHY is this happening? I didn't have the strength in me to fight the fight on top of everything else going on. I didn't resist him. I was just going to let him have his way.

Once he pulled his lips from my neck, he noticed my tears and saw that I was scared. He looked surprised. "I'm sorry, I thought…" He never finished his statement. "Let's go I'll take you home." He'd heard the rumors and believed I was one of the hot girls. I began wearing baggy jeans and a large sport jacket no matter what the temperature was outside. I didn't like my body and the attention it attracted. I wanted to hide my curves.

My tears wouldn't allow me to sleep that night. I fell into a deep state of depression. Why was all of this happening to me? How come nobody cared? I was alone and there seemed to be no one that I could talk to that understood me. Everyone had their preconceived notion of who I was and what I'd become. I couldn't justify living any longer. I didn't want to be a part of such an ugly cruel world. On my way to school the next morning, in a daze, I made yet another attempt to end my life. I stood bewildered at the bus stop, consumed by my negative thoughts. I believed everyone would be happier with me dead. Without any further thinking I closed my eyes and unconsciously stepped out into the street as the city bus approached. Time stood still. I inhaled deeply, awaiting the impact.

Nothing happened. I opened my eyes to see that the bus had come to a stop. It was only an inch or so away from my face – never touched me. The other people that were standing at the bus stop boarded the bus casually. It's like I was invisible. I thought maybe this is what happens right after you die. I pinched myself – I think I'm still alive. But how? I'd calculated the distance between the bus and the bus stop, and its speed perfectly so that the impact would have enough force to kill me instantly. I hadn't heard any rubber burning to indicate that the bus driver had to brake suddenly. It was like the moment never happened. But it did.

That moment convinced me of divine intervention. There was no other explanation. Something had shielded me from the destruction I sought. Something was protecting me. It wanted me to keep living. But why?

I thought back to the dream where the tornado had destroyed my life. Everything and everyone around me crumbled and fell under the pressure of the storm. Everything but me. I'd walked away unscathed. I'd been shaken up. My world was un ruins. The storm was the end of some things but not all things. It wasn't the end of me.

I stopped trying to defend my reputation to people who were determined to believe the worst about me. Before I could even think of doing something unbecoming of the young lady I should have been, people assumed I was already doing them anyway. I was being accused of things I'd never even considered doing. I figured I might as well just live up to my reputation but on my own terms. I'd succumb to some of those accusations.

It was awkward seeing the officer on campus at school. I never told anyone what happened, but it made my time at the school more uncomfortable. I wondered if everyone was thinking the same things about me. I was feeling more comfortable and the incident was behind me when one of the boys from the varsity football team asked me out on a date. He was one of the students that had nicknamed me "Dillard". He had dark brown skin. His hair was jet black and silky. He stood about 6 ft tall. Very lean. He was cute and I liked him, so I accepted.

He took me to the movies and afterwards he wanted to go on a walk at the park. How romantic, I thought. He pulled up at the park, but he didn't get out right away. He leaned over for a kiss. This kiss was consensual, I was in control and aware of what I was going to allow to happen that night. We moved to the back seat of his two-door car and continued making out. It was dark outside. I didn't notice when the other two boys approached the car. He opened the driver side door and stepped out of the car to let the other boys in while he stood watch outside. One boy joined me in the back and the other sat in the driver seat to await his turn.

"What is this? What's going on?" I backed into the farthest corner of the car.

"What's going on is, aint no fun if the homies can't have none." He proceeded to remove my clothes, but I started screaming and kicking him. With such little space in the car he couldn't get a good handle on me and quickly gave up. I was scared. It was three of them and one me. They didn't want any trouble, they too thought I was going to be okay with this. "Nah we can't do this, she's scared." I heard one of them speaking to me date. I was furious and demanded that he take me home.

I didn't want to go back to that school after that, so I started skipping with some girls that had adult friends with cars. These boys came in met us outside of the school yard gates and took us to their house in somewhere Coral Springs. I sat comfortably on the floor in front of the television watching Jerry Springer and other daytime talk shows the other girls were in the back having their way with the men. It was naive of me to think that these men would not try to have sex with me too.

"I know you didn't come over here to watch TV and eat Cheetos." One guy asked.

"Yep." I just wanted to get out of going to school.

"Your girls are in there fucking. You're going to have to fuck something too." Said another. I didn't respond. Just because the girls that I was with were in the back getting deep dish should not have been an implication that I was willing to do the same. I got up to go to the restroom. Before I could close the door one of the guys pushed it back open and proceeded to attack me. He was trying to get me down onto the floor, but I was not about to let that happen. Once again somebody was trying to violate my body and take away my right to choose. I was ready to die fighting, but he was going to take these punches and shed some blood for every boy or man that came before him. All my built-up rage and frustration gave me the strength I needed to defend myself. It was liberating to see him on the bathroom floor in pain.

I was able to escape and ran wasn't sure where we were exactly, but I'd notice that there was a bus stop outside. I decided to wait for the bus and tell the bus driver what I'd gotten myself into. I was hoping the bus driver would give me a free ride closer to home or at least tell me how to get there.

The girls that I was with came running out of the house. They were still fixing their clothes. "I'm so sorry about that, girl we told them not to mess with you." I don't know that I believed them, but I was happy to not be alone. "Fuck them", she declared. "I called my other friend. He is going to meet us at the gas station up the street."

At the gas station up the street waited another car full of boys. Here we go. This time I did hear the girls telling the guys that I'm not having sex and that no one was to touch me. The boys gave us a ride back to our side of town. They lived in the same condominium complex as my grandmother. I knew exactly where I was. It was still too early to go home, it was still school hours, I was stuck there listening to the bed banging and moaning as the girls served up yet another round of copulation.

In my days of rebellion, I'd made bad choices and put myself in situations that could have ended up more horribly than they did. I still didn't want to go back to that school. My grandmother didn't have the legal right to transfer me back to Dillard. Even if she did, there was no guarantee that things would be any different. If this is what it was going to be like to skip school every day I'd rather stay home. I would hide in the bushes outside my grandmother's condo. When my grandmother would leave to go off to work every morning, I'd go back inside. On the nights that she worked the night shift, I knew she'd be coming home around 9:30 the next morning and I'd have to find somewhere else to go. I'd met a girl in the condominium complex, she was 19 and finished with high school. She told her mom that I was 18, so her mom was okay with us hanging out. It gave me a safe place to spend my days when I couldn't go home.

My mother testified against me in court. She was on his side supporting him, calling me a liar. I was not allowed in the courtroom to hear her testimony nor the testimonies of the other witnesses. On the day that I was called to testify gramma had purchased me a pretty dress and she prayed with me before sending me off with my uncle. He drove me to the courthouse ranting about the bastard needing to be buried under the jail.

"You just get up there on that stand and you tell them what that bastard did to you." He was so angry and emotional, but I felt calm. I had no idea what I was walking into. No one had prepared me on what to expect. The Guardian ad litem assigned to my case had been unsuccessful in her attempts to reach me because my mom had not notified me that she was trying. My mom was trying to weaken the State's case against Alan.

I found out that I had been recommended for counseling, but it was cancelled because I never showed up. I never knew about it. I felt that I could have benefited from getting therapy after everything that had happened. It was frustrating to know that my own mother was deliberate in her attempts to sabotage me.

The trial had been going on for days, but I was meeting this woman for the first time. So much had happened since that day everything came out. My entire world had been shaken up and was falling apart. I was numb. I just wanted to get it over with.

I was called to the stand. I was going to have to be brave just a few moments longer. This was almost over. On my approach to take my seat I remember the words written on the piece of paper from my mother's room. "Make her tell the truth." Once seated, I had to swear to tell the truth, the whole truth, and nothing but the truth so helps me God.

The prosecutor questioned me first. She asked me to look around the room and see if I see the person who'd hurt me. I'd kept my eyes low and avoided making any contact with the other eyes in the room. There were so many. There was Alans family seated in the stands. I saw the two men that I ran to the night that he was arrested. I saw my uncle and then I saw him.

"Yes."

"Can you point him out?" I hesitated. Seeing him brought back all the darkness. He'd deprived me of my childhood. My hope for an absolution was replaced with the feelings of fear. "I just need you to point him out and you never have to look at him again." I pointed at Alan. We locked eyes; he shook his head in denial.

The prosecutor continued her line of questioning asking me why I'd stated that I'd been penetrated anally. I'm certain that as I explained my confusion, I left some other people confused. During questioning I also learned that Alan had been in prison before. He'd confessed to lewd and lascivious acts against a minor. He had sexually abused the son of an ex-girlfriend. He had just been released not long before he met my mom.

She was aware of his past convictions and believed him when he said that he was tricked into signing the confession papers. We'd been told that he did time for fighting in a bar. Still My mother was aware of his past, yet she allowed him to be in proximity with her 2 boys and 4 girls before she'd known him a month. How did she NOT believe me? She didn't *WANT* to believe. She'd come home to witness what she knew was a questionable situation. She MADE me go to work with him even when I'd begged her not to make me go. Now she was testifying as a witness for the accused in his case, her testimony went against me, her child. Having the mother of the alleged victim testify on your behalf and in condemning my testimony she helped his case.

"Make her tell the truth."

The defense attorney began her line of questioning. She wasn't very warm. Her questions were invasive and insensitive. She asked me very uncomfortable questions about my private parts and the humiliating details I'd rather have kept hidden. This in front of everyone in the room. Everyone in the room would hear, in my own words, a very detailed and descriptive account of the unfolding of events.

Still those words "Make her tell the truth." Resounded in my head.

"Did he ever put his penis in your mouth?" As uncomfortable as it was to have this information exposed. This was a time when I gave serious thought to what my mom said about recanting my story. I was embarrassed and uncomfortable having to disclose all of this in front of my family and his. I heard the words even louder. *Make her tell the truth.* I opened my mouth and hesitated. I wanted to lie but the truth came out. It happened More than once as the prosecution finished their line of questioning. Anytime I gave any hesitation or any thought to telling the truth. Anytime I wanted to lie my way through an embarrassing question, even if it was something, I hadn't been forthcoming about with the detectives. On the stand that day, I'd open my mouth and the truth always came out.

"Why didn't you tell anyone?" I didn't know how to answer that question. There were different reasons at different times all rooted in fear of what would happen if I did.

The jury deliberated and he was convicted of all charges. This included sexual battery against a minor and child abuse. He was sentenced to 5 terms of life in prison. A life sentence for each year of my life he'd taken away from me. The examiner's report from the sexual assault Treatment Center had revealed irrefutable evidence that supported my testimony. His semen was found in and around my vagina.

His conviction wasn't the end. It was just the beginning of the next series of storms. My relationship with my mother drifted further apart. She became more resentful and began to ignore my existence. I grew more resentment of her as well. There were undeniable things revealed in court still she blamed me for everything that had happened. I questioned her sanity and her integrity as a mother. Once she'd learned of the examiner's report, why was my mom so intentional in her attempts to dehumanize me and set him free? Why did she abandon me? I wondered how much of a difference it would have made had she supported me.

CHAPTER 12

"When we meet real tragedy in life, we can react in two ways. Either by losing hope and falling into self-destructive habits or by using the challenge to find our inner strength."

– Dalai Lama

I wanted to graduate high school. I'd have to work especially hard to graduate with my class and get my GPA up. I'd missed a lot of days and needed to repeat some classes to get my credits. The Varsity football players that tried to attack me were seniors and had graduated, and I would no longer need to cross paths with them at school. The school resource officer was still there. He, however, seemed to struggle with forgiving himself for violating me. It was equally as awkward for him having to see me at school. Both my silence and perseverance were punishment. He never bothered me again.

Still, my reputation preceded me. I had not done anything to silence the rumors. People believed what they wanted to believe. Stephanie had been in private school her whole life. Her parents had decided that a public high school experience would help to ground her culturally and socially. We grew very close very quickly. She was like a sister to me. If she'd heard anything, she didn't treat me according to what she'd heard. I never felt like she judged me based on anything she'd heard. Her father was like my second dad. Stephanie and her entire family were generous and kind to me. They allowed me into their home and invited me along whenever they'd have family outings. We had drama class together. For a project we choreographed a dance routine to Moulin Rouge. I don't think we were that good, but her dad was so supportive and encouraging. He and his girlfriend drove us to a Retirement Home where we proudly performed our routine for the residents.

Her parents were divorced. They shared custody of their three kids together. Her dad told me that he was homeless for a while after the divorce. He had literally been living on the streets under a bridge. The experience humbled him, it was his faith kept him strong, his kids were his reason to keep going. When he found work, he would ride his bike in all kinds of weather to get to work every day. He never gave up.

He took an interest in me and my future as if I were one of his daughters. College was a requirement in this family, not an option. He'd ask me what college I planned to attend. I hadn't given any thought to college in a while. My life had been such a distraction. I just wanted to finish high school. It was motivation, however, that he believed college to be in my future. I started to believe it too.

Back at school I was asked out by Malcolm. He was a senior on the basketball team. He was a class clown, always cracking jokes and creating distractions but he made me laugh. We'd been going out only a week when he introduced me to his mother. That's how I found how he was 20 years old. That explained the beard and the mustache. I was only 15.

Once we were alone, she was very direct with me. "You need to leave my son alone. You deserve better." I wondered why she would speak negatively against her son. She knew her son and was trying to keep me from getting hurt. Not to mention we were 5 years apart in age. Our involvement as boyfriend and girlfriend would not be socially acceptable.

After a year the bank had foreclosed on our house and my mom had to move out. By then the house was nothing worth saving. Everything was destroyed. My mom seemed to have given up on life. She did nothing to make herself look or feel good. It was as if her soul was tied to Allen and with him gone, she wouldn't give herself permission to be happy again…

perhaps she didn't think she was worthy of it.

She moved into a 2-bedroom duplex apartment a few miles east of the house we once called home. One bedroom was for her and the other was for Tootie and Angel. Dee was living with the man who fathered my first nephew, her now husband, but they visited frequently. My older brother had gone to live with my dad so that left 4 of us still under her care. I was lucky to ever get a spot on the couch. She unapologetically gave verbal confirmation that she did not want me there and didn't care where I slept. She wanted me to leave and was determined to make my living conditions so uncomfortable that I would do just that.

I'd overheard her in conversation introducing herself to our new neighbor. She described me as the one she should have aborted. She didn't realize the window was open and spoke loudly enough for me to hear those inner thoughts I'd always known existed but tried to ignore. They'd shown in her actions toward me. I listened to her give an account of how I'd seduced her man and was having sex with him and every other boy on the block. She said I lied and accused her man of rape causing him to life in prison and her life to fall apart. Hearing her say those things about me was both hurtful and infuriating but I wasn't surprised. She was going to extremes to victimize herself and characterize me as some wild promiscuous teenager. The churlish ingrate that cursed her life.

Adding insult to injury, I was no longer friends with Stephanie. She'd been added to the list of people in my life who would eventually do something to hurt me. Her mother lived in a luxurious apartment near the mall. She'd invited me to spend the weekend with them and was just as welcoming as Stephanie's dad. Her parents lived completely opposite lives like they come from different sides of the tracks so to speak. She was more established, poised, and successful. Her presence was almost intimidating, but she was a soft spoken, petite little lady.

We'd spent the day at the mall just hanging out with Stephanie's best cousin, Mia. She and Mia were as thick as thieves. Mia didn't like that Tiffany and I were so close. She wanted her cousin to herself. Together they would go off and do things without me. Stephanie was acting funny as well. They intentionally separated themselves from me. They didn't include me in their jokes and conversations. It made me feel bad. I wasn't trying to replace their relationship, I wanted to add to it. I was surprised as I had never known Stephanie to behave that way toward me.

Some good did come out of that afternoon at the mall. We'd gone into the salon at the mall for Stephanie to get her hair washed when a man came in wanting his hair braided. The salon owner advised him that there was no braider available, she was looking for one, and nobody knew how to braid. She was about to turn him away when Stephanie interrupted.

"Tiffany can do it!"

The owner asked if I were any good. Stephanie nodded, she recommended me with a smile. It took me about 30 minutes to cornrow the man's hair. The owner charged him $45 and gave me $20 of it. She thanked me for taking the client and told me to come back when I get my license. I'd made $20 in 30 minutes. I did the math, that was a potential $90 an hour if I cut out the middleman. In that moment I realized my true earning potential if I monetized my talent. I'd be the richest girl in 11th grade. I'd been charging $10 - $20 for my services, even braiding for free.

That night I was playing a board game with Stephanie's little sister. I took a break from the game and went to find Stephanie and Mia sitting on the stairs talking about me. They didn't notice me standing behind them. Mia laughed as Stephanie said how annoying I was and that she was only being nice to me because she felt bad that my mother didn't love me. I gave Stephanie and her cousin their space after that. They'd both noticed that I was withdrawn but it wasn't until after Mia went home with her mom that Stephanie asked why. I didn't tell her what I heard. I couldn't form the words. My heart was so broken I couldn't bring myself to repeat them. I silently withdrew myself as her friend.

I had nowhere else to go. I'd grown to resent my grandmother for her mistreatment and lies during my stay with her. She'd pretended to be my refuge from my mother but was also secretly in support of her daughter who'd gone to extremes to dehumanize me. She loved having a front row seat to the drama with my mother. I was determined to never go back there. Her scandalous lifestyle and decades of secrets made her an attention seeking paranoid. She seemed to enjoy gossip and talking about everyone else when their closet deeds were exposed. My presence gave me an eyewitness account to her secrets. Risking the exposure made her apprehensive about what I might see but I never shared her personal business with anyone. At this point, there was no one that I felt I could trust. As uncomfortable as I was with living with my mom, I felt that I could handle her. There was no question to her feelings toward me. She didn't pretend to love me or want me around, she let it be known that she didn't. She also knew she was wrong therefore she would rather make life for me so miserable that I would willingly leave. She could continue to paint me as a troubled teen heading down a path to destruction. But she was harmless. I would just continue to evade going home until after she'd fallen asleep to circumvent any conflict.

My plan worked most of the time but eventually we'd cross paths. Anytime we were in the same room together for too long things would get explosive. This would mostly happen on the weekends. Everything I did annoyed her, even my presence. I didn't help the situation any. I was angry with her and felt abandoned. I hated her for betraying her responsibilities as a mother. I started to become more vocal about my lack of respect for her. The rage I'd been holding back for years was flowing from my tongue like word vomit of the worst kind, but I didn't care to stop it. I'd been silenced for too long.

Marcus and I were no longer dating. My conversations with his mom helped me to recognize that I should want better for myself. She was real. I respected her for her authenticity. She'd seen beyond my pain and my fears and spoke directly to the core of who I was. I continued to attend church services with Ms. Avis on Sundays. She continued to listen and mentor me. She too had experienced sexual abuse in her youth. She showed me that there is life beyond the pain, but I couldn't achieve it alone. I needed to surrender to a higher power and go to God in prayer. I tried meditating but it was hard for me to silence my thoughts.

I was almost 16 years old, legally I was able to get a job. I could purchase my school clothes with the money I made so that's what I did. After school I'd walk a quarter of a mile to the retirement home around the corner from my school. It was a luxurious senior retirement community. The residents would come down to the dining room for a 3-course dinner beginning at 4pm. They'd placed their orders for appetizers from their rooms so we would already know what they wanted. Some of them ordered the same thing. We needed to set the tables, sit out their drinks and serve their appetizers hot and fresh. They received first class dining treatment. Child labor laws restricted how many hours I could work but once the schedule was set no one paid any attention to that. They just wanted the job done. Holidays were especially gracious. I would work overtime and get my biggest paychecks. The residents gave generous gifts to their favorite servers. Sometimes the gifts were monetary. I saw death there on many occasions during my first-year tenure.

Dee and her husband lived with his mom and his younger brother who was about my age. Sometimes I'd go over there to get a break from my mom. My relationship with my older sister was still very distant and undefined. Sometimes I'd feel like we were growing closer and then something would happen to reopen the wounds. When it came to me and my mother, she played both sides.

I answered the phone while visiting Dee one day and my mom thought I was her. I didn't correct her when she called me Dee. I was just playing around and continued as if I were the daughter, she thought I was. My mom referred to me as *that thing* and said to make sure I didn't see the stink perfume. "Hide it somewhere so she doesn't see it." As she was talking, I spotted the expensive bottle of perfume I'd purchased for my mom as a Mother's Day gift. It was right there on the dresser. She'd given it away to Dee. I just responded with, "okay", and hung up the phone. I didn't bother putting the perfume away.

Once the neighborhood boys learned of the new family of mostly girls moving in, they were all very welcoming. I did have a crush on this one guy, his name was Geek. He was old enough to drive and had his own car which to me at the time made him a man. He would come over and help around the house and do anything my mother asked. His chances with me were ruined when he lied, bragged to some friends about having sex with me. Enraged, I confronted him in front of everyone and made him tell the truth. Then I chased him down the street with a cast iron skillet from my mother's kitchen. He apologized but the damage was done. I despised him after that.

Another neighborhood boy, Thomas, was playing basketball at the park with his friend Mike when I met him. Mike was light skinned and corny, but he was smart and played basketball well. He had nice legs, but I was mostly attracted to his intellect. He spoke about a life in a philosophical way. He challenged me intellectually and used big words I'd never heard before. I'd have to use context clues to figure out the meaning of his words and keep up with his conversation. His hair cut in an afro like Kobe Bryant – my celebrity crush at the time. I was intrigued by him and saw him as someone I could learn from. Mike was visiting Thomas while on summer break from Howard University. He and I were very different but grew to be very close. He thought I was mean. Eventually he had to leave and return to school. We lost contact over time, but our short time together reminded me that there is still some good in the world.

CHAPTER 13

"Having courage does not mean that we are unafraid. Having courage and showing courage means we face our fears. We are able to say, "I have fallen but I will get up.""

– **Maya Angelou**

Dee's marriage ended in divorce before my nephew turned 2 years old and she was able to spend a lot more time around the house. This meant I'd lose my unofficial residency on the couch to her and the baby. I enjoyed having my nephew around but Dee not so much. She and I fought constantly. It was usually stemmed from a fight I'd have with my mom. Dee found my tone and word choice to be disrespectful and would always jump into our arguments to take her side. She wasn't a sister to me any more than my mother was a mom. In my mind it further reminded me of how alone I was in the world.

It got to the point where my mom would call my sister whenever she wanted to pick a fight with me and knew she wouldn't win. With all the anger and resentment, I had built up inside of me I can now understand why my actions toward her would seem belligerent. In hindsight it was probably scary. I hated my life, I hated my mom, I hated my siblings, I hated my school. The only thing I loved was anything and anyone that took me away from that place of misery. This sometimes meant making irresponsible choices that endangered my life.

Dee had a new friend, Chasity that I couldn't stand because she was dramatic and self-centered. My biggest gripe was because she referred to Dee as her sister. That was MY sister and I didn't like that they were closer as friends than Dee and I were as actual sisters. Her presence ended up being a blessing to our relationship because my jealousy helped me to put aside my resentment for my sister and start over. Dee and I became closer because of her.

The pivotal moment for me was when I owned my contribution to my own brokenness. At this point I began to see how my attitude had made me unpleasant to be around. It was me. I was angry at the world. My negative thinking, self-loathing, and victimization made me mean and unapproachable. Though justifiable considering my circumstances, I had the power to change my thoughts and ultimately my perspective on life. I stopped expecting to find happiness in tomorrow and realized that I could decide to be happy today. I can't change the past. I have no control over my mother or the other people I felt mistreated or abused me or treated me unfairly. If I continue to live my life would certainly entail of a plethora of other injustices and difficult people. I would certainly feel misunderstood again.

I had a choice to continue feeling like a victim, revisiting the past and sulking in the darkness. Or I could forgive. Forgive my mother for not protecting me. Forgiving the people who didn't believe me. Forgive my sibling for not supporting me and everyone that I felt abandoned me in my time of need. Most importantly I needed to forgive myself. I'd sat lost in the darkness for far too long. I don't remember who it was that first introduced me to "The Celestine Prophecy" by James Redfield but as much as it helped me to heal some spiritual wounds it contradicted my religious beliefs.

Chasity was a pretty girl but extremely insecure about her skin condition that left spots all over her legs. Her brother was a popular football player at my high school, but I never really knew anything about him other than his name. He went pro and had a very successful career. Her appeal and promiscuity gained her the attention of the ballers which is how I was able to get into the 21+ clubs at 16 years old.

Being inside a club at 16 years old was invigorating but scary at times. The men were aggressive, grabbing my arm and my behind demanding attention. They didn't take rejection well and were likely to pour their drink in your face or try to fight you if you refused their advances. Chasity protected me like her little sister and would go off any time she noticed a man making me feel uncomfortable but there were times I'd have to handle it myself. Guys would get very disrespectful. They assumed that your presence at the club meant you were aware of the nature and wanted that type of attention.

I saw a lot of things happening in and around the club. People would get drunk and fight over someone stepping on their shoes. A man was shot just feet away from me. It was the first time I saw someone die. Gun fights were not at all uncommon and would happen often.

On the stage were girls dancing dressed in lingerie' or cropped tops and short skirts. One night at the club the audience watched in enjoyment as three men took turns sexually penetrating one woman on stage. She may have been high on some drugs at the time, but she seemed to enjoy having a penis in her mouth and in her vagina at the same time. It started off as suggestive dancing but quickly escalated to an orgy on stage. Outside the club was like an extension of the party going on inside. Once the club closed people would walk or drive around in the parking lot just to be seen. People would be having sex in cars, drinking and smoking. That was where guys would fish to see who they'd be taking home.

I enjoyed dancing and having a good time, but the club was never my scene. It was just something to do. So, when Chasity met a man that invited her and her friends to ride up to Mississippi for a few days, I was on board. It was me, Chasity and Dee along with the man, his son and his nephew. We knew nothing about these men and had no money if something happened, but we jumped at the opportunity to take a road trip out of the state.

It was a plethora of irresponsible choices and an opportunity for so much to go wrong but these men, although a little weird, turned out to be harmless. I'm not sure what Chasity said or did to that old man, but he paid for everything we wanted and took very good care of us. I was to keep the nephew, Melvin, occupied and Dee was entertainment for the son.

Melvin and I got to know each other quite a bit during the 13-hour drive to Biloxi. He had just turned 18 years old a few weeks prior. He had a milk chocolate complexion and a complete gentleman. He had a real think country accent. I thought it was cute. He was extremely smart, an aspiring engineer and was going to begin his freshman year of college in the fall.

Chasity was a certified pimp. She had the old man wrapped around her fingers. She told him whatever he wanted to hear and seduced him with her words.

Dee, however, got the short end of the hillbilly stick. Her designated beau was obsessed with her curves, but she was clearly grossed out by the mere sight of him. Her face said everything her words didn't express but he was persistent. He enjoyed the chase. It was pure entertainment for the rest of us.

During our two day stay on the farm we enjoyed farm life very much. We got up early in the morning to feed the animals and groom the horses. I remembered visiting Tradewinds Park with my dad when I was younger. I always loved when he'd take us horseback riding. The old man told us not to make the horses run when we ride them, but Chasity was special. She wanted to see what would happen. She and I were on the horse together one minute and the in the next minute I was flying. I landed hip first on a stack of hay. I looked over in the direction of the horse and saw him about to lower his front legs on top of Chasity's hear. She rolled out of his path just in time.

Melvin came running over to help me up, but I could barely walk. I was in tears and Chasity was cracking up laughing at her near-death experience. He carried me to the house and examined my hip for any signs of broken bones. It was badly bruised but not broken. I would need to rest in bed for the duration of the night. Melvin helped me into the shower and washed my body like a baby. He had the perfect set of lips and knew how to use them. Once in the bedroom, he laid me down and kissed my hips. Besides being a good kisser, his cunnilingus skills were impeccable.

No one questioned me about where we were and who we'd been with once we got back home. It was like no one even noticed. When I wasn't hanging out with Dee and Chasity, I was down the street at my friend Kimora's house. She was one of my classmates at William Dandy and then at Dillard, but she was still determined to graduate, and I had given up. Kimora was one of 10 kids in her household but there was a distinct difference about her. She had a deeply rooted love for Jesus Christ and prayed constantly just as the Bible had commanded.

As a neighbor and friend of the family I formed relationships with Kimora's extended family. I started dating her cousin, Kevin, who was also a classmate, but he was a year ahead of us and had moved away to Clearwater with his mom. He came home to visit that summer and asked me out. Our relationship would be mostly long distance because he lived in Clearwater and would be going to play football for a college in North Carolina in the fall. I told him I'd call and visit him as much as I could, and he promised the same. Her sister, Martha was older than us and could drive. She taught me how to flat wrap my hair and get it all bouncy and voluminous. I'd hang out in the streets with her and her friends all day while Kimora was at school, but Kimora would rarely hang out with us even at night. We'd often end up in situations that went against her beliefs.

Every summer we'd all take the city bus down to the beach and spend the entire day there. Martha was a great cook. She would season the meats and we'd have a barbeque. We wouldn't head home until the sun went down. Kevin and I connected through our traumas which were similar. He had been molested and sexually abused by his mother. He was forced to perform sexually for his mother who justified the abuse as her determination to make him a real man. He was so young and so broken. I identified with his brokenness and wanted to help him heal. I believed that we could heal each other and be each other's peace.

Martha could be seen coming up the street but her belligerent shouting preceded her. She was on her way to our house to fight Dee's friend, Chasity, and she had her entire family behind her. Chasity had committed the crime of not being afraid of Marsha and something had to be done about that.

The family of 10 crowded around Chasity taunting her. Trying to intimidate her. She seemed bothered and unbothered at the same time. It's hard to identify the source of the beef between Marsha and Chasity. They never got along from the first time they met. Martha was a bully and Chasity was sarcastic and rude. Neither was afraid of the other, but Chasity wasn't confrontational. Once Marsha decided that she wanted blood there was nothing anyone could say or do to stop her from attacking.

She met her match that day. Martha threw the first punch and missed. Chasity returned fire and in the next moment they were throwing punches on the asphalt in the middle of the road. Martha must've believed this was going to be an easy win because she came to the fight wearing a dress with no underwear and no bra. All her glory was exposed. There was a car coming up the street that was halted by the sexy brawl. Chasity was dragging Martha by her hair and tried to toss her in front of the oncoming car. The driver frantically got out of her car to break up the fight. Martha's walk back home included a bloody face and ripped clothing while Chasity appeared unscathed, but Martha continued her banter.

My dad came over to visit one day as I was reading the Celestine Prophecy for the 2nd time. I invited him to share his perspective. His cognitive dissonance wouldn't allow him to interpret the book as anything other than the devil's work. I hadn't had an opportunity to really talk with my dad after what happened. I'm convinced the conversation would been awkward for him, but we never discussed the details of what happened. He never asked and I didn't volunteer to share. We mutually avoided the topic all together wanting only to move forward with our relationship. Something about the way he hugged me was a reminder of his love. They served as the words that went unspoken. I missed getting hugs and kisses from my dad but now any time I wanted to spend time with him at his house he'd always say, "I have to ask my wife." I respected him for wanting to protect the sanctity of his marriage, but it sounded more like a cop out. He didn't want to be the one to say, no.

My dad was the one that encouraged me to withdraw from public school and join Job Corps. I'd be able to earn my high school diploma and take up a trade at the same time. This would've been my sophomore year in high school. I would've preferred to withdraw from Boyd Anderson and finish at Dillard, but I'd fallen so far behind in my credits for missing so many days. I chose to attend the Job Corps in Asheville, North Carolina which was only a few hours' drive from where Kevin attended college. I saw it as an opportunity to right my wrongs and turn my life around. He sat with me through the orientation and enrollment then a week later he was driving me to the airport to bid me farewell.

At Job Corps I met personalities from all over the US. My roommates were Melody from New York, Megan from Alabama, and Porsha from South Carolina. Melody was the loud outspoken one. She was never short on words. She shared that she'd secretly gotten her vulva pierced and how it made her orgasms more explosive. Megan was a timid white girl from Alabama. She was raised in trailer parks but had the humblest spirit. Porsha wasn't the oldest of our crew, but she was by far the most mature. We all learned a lot from each other. We'd stay up at night braiding each other's hair, doing our nails and facials. We shared our stories and experiences as well as our tears. We formed a sisterhood and promised to keep in touch but unfortunately, we lost touch. Porsha and Melody had chosen masonry as their trade. I'd chosen Business Clerical. Porsha graduated just months after I arrived. She'd been there two years already and wasn't at all excited to go back home. Melody got kicked out for fighting. They had a zero-tolerance policy for fighting that conflicted with Melody's zero tolerance for human beings. Their presence was replaced by two other young ladies. One from Mississippi and another from Miami, not far from where I lived in Ft. Lauderdale.

A counselor at The Job Corp facility, after reviewing the results of my practice test, proposed that I might be able to graduate early. They were changing the high school equivalency tests to a GED test and based on my scores she believed I'd be able to complete the program before this transition happened. If I passed, I'd only need to finish my trade program and then I could graduate. I passed after the first attempt and was excited to be completing the program early and earning my high school diploma. Something which I'd recently thought to be too far out of reach was now in the palm of my hands.

TIFFANY YOUNG

CHAPTER 14

I'd tried reaching out to Kevin by phone a few times, but my attempts were unsuccessful. When I first arrived at Job Corps, he'd write letters to me wishing me luck and telling me he missed me. Over the next few months the flow of letters decreased until they'd stopped completely. By the time I'd finished the program he'd gotten consumed by college life – and college girls.

When I returned home to Florida, I heard that he'd been baker acted. He had been doing drugs with some of his college friends and started hallucinating. He was saying that God was speaking to him, telling him to kill his mother. Hearing about his condition did not prepare me for the next time I'd see him. I could hardly recognize him. He was missing teeth; his clothes were torn and dirty. He looked homeless. If he was homeless, I'm sure that was a decision he'd come to on his own because his family would not just put him out on the streets like that. Unless his condition was worse than I thought, and he'd become violent. But Kevin was a gentle giant, I just couldn't image him being violent. I was driving around in our old neighborhood at night when I spotted him. I called his name, still not 100% sure it was Kevin, but it was.

"Kevin?" I called to him. He turned around and smiled squeamishly. He wasn't sure who I was.

"Who is that?" He spoke slowly and in a distressed voice I didn't recognize. Something was wrong. This wasn't the Kevin I knew. He was incoherent.

"It's me, Tiffany."

"Hey Tiffany." I exited the car and went over to hug him. I was disturbing to see him in that state when the last time I'd seen him he was completely functional. That was the last time I'd see him before Kimora's funeral. Kimora and I were close, I had no idea she was having suicidal thoughts. I had no idea she was depressed. I never imagined she of all people would take her own life. She was always the one that would minister to everyone and encourage them. She was a believer. A warrior for Christ, a prayer warrior. Martha was the one that found her with a self-inflicted gunshot wound to her head. She shared with me that Kimora had begun having blackouts after giving birth to her daughter. The doctors could not figure out why. She had just purchased her first home and was pregnant with her second child when she learned that the father of her child, her boyfriend, had married another woman. On top of that, her employment status as a deputy with the Sheriffs' Office was threatened by her medical condition which had no diagnosis. She was determined unfit for duty after having an episode while on the job. She didn't qualify for disability because doctors couldn't find anything wrong with her. Kimora had shared these things with me before, but she seemed to be maneuvering well. She'd invited me to her housewarming. I couldn't make it. That would have been the last time I saw her, but I didn't go. I regret that I couldn't read through her seemingly well put together. She was always praying and helping people through their problems I never thought of her as having any of her own that she couldn't pray herself through.

After Job Corps I decided to join the military. Daddy took me to the recruitment center near his house. I'd been staying with him and his family once I returned. They enjoyed having me there because I was always cooking. I wasn't the best cook, but I would find recipes and try them out using whatever ingredients I could match in their kitchen. Sometimes the food came out nasty, daddy put hot sauce on it and ate it anyway. He would moan and make noises like it was the best tasting nasty food he'd ever had.

I was walking to the corner store one day purchasing cigarettes for my mom when I was approached by Prince. He was very handsome with fair complexion and silky hair. He described himself as a Jamaican Indian, but he didn't have an accent. He'd been born and raised in the states. His family lived in New York. He had moved to Florida with his mom and was contemplating going back home.

I was so guarded after love had failed me so many times. I wasn't sure I even believed in it anymore at this point. I rejected his invitation to go out on a date. He insisted that I take his number and we could just be friends. We hung out quite a bit. I frequently visited my new friend at his apartment in North Lauderdale. The first time I stayed overnight he was a complete gentleman and did not make any sexual advances. The next time I stayed he was a bit more aggressive. He did not continue his advances beyond my stern, "NO". It did, however, seem to be a bruise to his ego. He was confused. He wasn't expecting to get rejected after we'd been spending time together and having so much fun over three months. He was doing everything right. He would bring me food when I was hungry and took me shopping at the mall. He'd drive me to the laundry mat to do my laundry every week and even helped me fold. One night at the laundry mat he ran into a friend who asked him about his daughter. The guy called him out by name. They shook hands and exchanged hugs, but Prince didn't have a daughter.

"What? Daughter? Man, you're crazy get out of here. You got the wrong guy." Prince laughed at the crazy encounter. After months of hanging out, sleeping in the bed together and never having sex he was confused. He started to question if I was gay or a stripper. The stripper theory came from a t-shirt I had from a local strip club. It wasn't even my shirt. It belonged to Dee, but I'd wear it to bed sometimes. He was reaching trying to figure out why I was holding back from him. He was growing on me I just couldn't allow myself to be vulnerable and express that to him. I didn't share my past experiences with him, but I asked him to be patient with me and he didn't give up. He waited until I was ready. We made love for the first time and I shared with him over pillow talk that I'd be leaving for the military soon. The disappointment was written all over his face. He gave me an ultimatum and told me that if I leave for the military, we were over. I'd made the decision to do what I wanted to do despite how anyone else felt. I would not be distracted by any relationship that could end again at any moment.

My relationship with my father was being restored as if nothing had ever happened. Instead of starting over we just picked up where we left off. I didn't blame him for anything, and I was only a little bit disappointed that he had not fought for his right to be in our lives. I wasn't resentful though. I understood. I was just happy to have him around. To hug me and to hear him call me his Princess again.

"You got your daddy face but your mama's everything else." My daddy's friends gave me creeper vibes. Even going to church with him I felt eyes watching my behind when I walked. These were saved holy men, but I knew better than to believe that they were without sin. I could feel the spirit of perversion and their dirty thoughts that said what their eyes did not. It made me uncomfortable. I scored very high on my ASVAB and had enlisted as a Morse Interceptor for the Army, but I almost didn't make it in. My BMI was too high. I measured in at 5'5" and 150lbs. I needed to lost weight. My recruiter ran with me every day for 2 weeks, gave me a meal plan and helped me to get to where I needed to be.

He helped me open my first bank account where I could set up my direct deposit. He also offered me some advice, "The drill sergeants are paid to do a job just like any other employee. Don't take it personally when they yell and scream at you. They're just doing their job. They go home to have dinner with their families at night just like normal people." I was grateful for him and all his advice. It sure did help when I went to bootcamp. The moment the new recruits stepped off the bus into the mud there were drill sergeants lined up shouting about how they were going to break us down and toughen us up. They all used their outside voices even when we weren't outside. It was entertaining to me because I knew their secret thanks to my trusty recruiter.

After 911 there were rumors of wars and rumors that our training would be cut short and we'd be sent into battle. I was getting all my information from the other soldiers in my platoon whenever they'd communicate with their friends and families. We didn't have any television and minimal contact with the outside. I was scared. I thought about how I'd only recently begun to want to live. I was enjoying life. I wanted to eventually be a wife and a mother. I realized I was not willing to die for this country. I spoke to my superior officer about what I was feeling.

"Well no one wants to fight alongside somebody who doesn't want to be here. Give yourself a day to think about it and if you still want to leave, I'll discharge you." Her response shocked me because it was understood that once you're in you can never get out. It was now or never. I decided the military wasn't for me. It was best that I take this opportunity to get out and go back home.

Not much else had changed back home. I hadn't heard from Prince the entire time I was in the Army and he wasn't accepting any of my calls. I was only able to reach him through his cousin Ahmad. I ran into Ahmad when shopping at the mall. He informed me that Prince had changed his telephone number and moved back to New York. I asked if he would call him for me. I wanted to speak to him.

I wasn't expecting Prince to agree to speak to me, but he did. I'd assumed he was still upset. He was happy to hear from me and invited me to join him in New York. He booked me flight for a few days later and I went to join him. He was there waiting for me at the airport with a smile on his face. I was happy to see him. Then he dropped a bomb on me. He has a 3-year-old daughter back in Florida living with her mom; his ex-girlfriend. The crazy guy at the laundry mat was telling the truth. He apologized for lying to me about something so miniscule. He went on to explain that was keeping her from me because he thought I wouldn't be with him if I knew he had a kid. Now that I would be meeting his family, he knew I'd eventually find out. He was worried that one of his family members might think I was the baby's mother and ask about the baby. He'd then have to explain that I'm not, I'm his girlfriend. He didn't want me to find out that way. He wanted to protect me from the awkward moment.

I needed time to process this new information. I had so many questions. I wasn't at all upset that he had a kid, I was disappointed that he denied her. I thought about how I'd felt had my father denied my existence. I'd be hurt. I wondered what type of person he thought I was. For him to think I wouldn't want to date him because he has a daughter, did he really believe I was that person. Why would you want to date someone like that? It was hard not to question everything else I thought I knew about him. What other lies has he told?

My imagination was taking over my thoughts. I needed to regain control and avoid overthinking or jumping to conclusions. He made a mistake. He is now trying to make it right. Just go with it.

I told him that I wanted to meet her. He explained that he and his daughter's mother did not get along since the relationship ended. She was bitter and did not allow him to see his daughter at all. My emotions changed from disappointment to sympathy and I forgave the small infraction.

He proposed to me that night on the streets of Long Island New York. It was a cold November night. We were just walking and sightseeing when he took my hand and dropped down on one knee. Thanksgiving was a week away, but the streets were already decorated with holiday lights. I would have cried tears of joy, but my tear ducts were frozen. Even after spending a year in the mountains of North Carolina, my Florida blood had not conformed to in that kind of cold. I said, yes.

I'd adapted within a couple of weeks but if I were going to live there in Long Island with Prince, I needed to find a job. Prince was not at all happy to hear that I'd decided to work. He didn't want me to work. Somehow, he'd associated me working with me meeting other men. I'd never given him a reason to think I would cheat on him; he was being insecure. I thought it was cute. Nonetheless, I was determined to find a way to make this work for the both of us. I was not at all comfortable with the thought of living off him and his parents. I wanted to contribute. I knew the perfect place. There was a mall in walking distance from where we lived with Prince's father. I could work there part time while Prince was at work. He would think I was shopping which wouldn't be far from the truth. It was a fool proof plan.

I filled out several applications and was hired by Macys. I was only working there for a week before I got caught. Prince was livid. He found my Macy's ID still attached to a top I'd worn that day. I'm not good at coming up with extemporaneous stories. I'm more comfortable telling the truth and accepting the consequences. He forbade me returning to work. We argued for days about how controlling he was being. He'd been complaining about the phone bill being too high from me making long distance calls to my sister back home in Florida. I was home all day with nothing to do but talk on the phone. I didn't know anyone in New York. I was wrong for deceiving him, but he was being uncompromising. I didn't want to argue about money. I didn't want to be a liability. I didn't want to be controlled.

Ultimately, I would submit to his demands and quit my job. I was miserable. The only time I got out of the house was if I took a walk to the mall or Prince would take be with him to roam the streets after he got off work. Prince's father did all the cooking. My cooking was too bland for his Jamaican taste buds. He needed spice. He noticed that I was growing more miserable and did things to try to make me feel more at home. Shopping was the one thing he knew I'd enjoy but I grew bored with that as well. A trip to the local Syms for a new suit was the final straw. I was briefly distracted by a nice car on our approach to enter the store. Prince and I were holding hands. Before I could speak a word, Prince snatched his hand away from me.

"Why don't you go jump in the car with him then?" Prince assumed I was looking at the driver of the car. I didn't even notice there was someone in the driver seat. I just thought it was a nice car. I was looking at the car not the man.

There was nothing I could say to convince Prince of this. He threatened to leave me at the store and make me find my way back home. I wasn't sure if he was serious, but it was disturbing to hear. Why would you leave me in the middle of nowhere? I have no one to call. No money because he wouldn't allow me to work. I was solely dependent on him. He'd placed a block on the phone so that I could not exceed 30 minute of talk time on the phone with my sister each month. I apologized to keep the peace but was adamant that I was not looking at the man. He didn't believe me. The remainder of the shopping trip was unpleasant. I remained silent until we arrived back at his dad's.

"I want to go home." I admitted. He was shocked to hear me say I wanted to leave him.

"For how long?" He asked

"Just a week or so. I just need some time to think." I lied. I had no plans to return to him after the way that he'd embarrassed me and threatened to leave me at the store. However, I knew that if I'd told him that he'd never purchase my ticket back home.

"You trying to leave me now? You think I'm crazy?" He was smiling when he said that. I wasn't deceived. I knew he was crazy.

CHAPTER 15

Getting reacclimated to life in Florida wasn't hard but getting reacclimated to love was. I wasn't interested in falling in love, but the idea of love was still very much alive inside of me. I met Keisha through some other acquaintances that lived in our neighborhood and nearby areas. My loyalty wasn't to any one hood or another. I just hated going home so I stayed in the streets to avoid it.

After my relationship with Prince ended so abruptly. I was disillusioned that it had failed without and real closure. At times I questioned my decision to leave him. He was good to me. He was extremely jealous and potentially obsessive but that just meant his love for me was deep, right? He did lie about his daughter but that was because he didn't want to lose me. Everyone tells little white lies when they first meet people. It's because they don't want anyone to judge them before really getting to know them. Was I being a brat?

I tried calling him a few times, but he'd stopped answering my calls. Listening to India Arie's album "Ready for Love" I would think about finding love again, but I wasn't in any hurry. I wanted my next man to be my husband. I knew that would take time and perhaps divine intervention. I always knew that I wanted to be a wife and mother. Spending time in New York with Prince gave me a taste of being domesticated and what it would be like if I were married. I prayed and told myself that the next guy I dated with a car, his own place, and respect for his mother I would give love a chance and stick it out no matter what happened. I would commit and I wouldn't run away.

My season of friendship with Keisha brought me back to the neighborhood where I grew up. I avoided the street where my childhood home once stood. It brought back too many painful memories I'd work hard on forgetting. Like a house of horrors.

Keisha had a baby girl about 1 year old, but she lived at home with her mom. She wasn't ready to be a mom and released her frustrations on the child physically and verbally. She left her baby in the crib for the better part of each day only taking her out if we had somewhere to go and no one to watch the baby. She was dating one of the boys from the neighborhood, but he wasn't the father of her daughter. They fought a lot, almost daily. Arguments would always turn violent between the two. The biological father wanted nothing to do with her romantically. His parents, however, were a big help to Keisha and her daughter's needs. Keisha was always happy when her daughter went to visit with the grandparents.

Keisha's boyfriend, Kevin, came over to visit frequently. Her house was one of the neighborhood hangouts. We'd be up all-night playing spades, drinking and smoking. I'd only participate in the card games, but I found it entertaining to watch everyone get drunk and start behaving foolishly.

"Keisha, if you had a body and a brain like Tiffany, I'd NEVER cheat on you." Her boyfriend announced his attraction to me during a game of spades after he'd had way too much to drink. There was an awkward moment of silence across the room. I felt everyone's eyes turn to look for my reaction, but I starred extra hard at the cards in my hand, avoiding eye contact and pretended not to hear him. The silence was broken by what we'd naturally expected her reaction to be - a slap to his face. That slap lead to a simulation of a violent prison brawl. This was the most violent of fights I'd ever seen between the couple. She was obviously deeply hurt by his words and used her hands to express this. He returned with punches to her face and anything else readily available for the impact of his fists. When she fell to the floor, they began kicking each other. No one stepped in to break up the fight. They would fight so much we all knew not to intervene because they would both turn on whomever tried to be the peace maker.

Our queue to intervene was when they both grew weary. We'd know they were tired because the punching and hitting slowed down and they'd be stuck together looking like the character "Cat-Dog" while pulling each other's hair.

His friends took him away in their car while she and I went inside to get her cleaned up.

"What's going on between you and Kevin?" Her line of questioning felt more like she was insinuating. All a sudden, I was a suspect.

"Girl, what?" I was offended.

"Are you fucking my man?" I wanted to say how grossly unattractive he was not just physically, but he was a broke nigga from the hood. He had no class, no car and no money. Not my type.

"Don't nobody want your man but you, boo." I thought this was a nicer way to express my lack of interest without jeopardizing our friendship. "Ima' just leave before you piss me off."

"Good. Bye" Her face was starting to swell, and blood leaked from the open wounds on her skin, but her ego was bruised.

I was sleeping in my cousin's old bedroom at my aunt Lyn's house just two blocks away. All but one of her kids were grown and she allowed me to stay there. It was rent free at first but once I started working for the local telecommunications company, she was asking for $300 a month. I agree that this was fair even though between my enrollment into Beauty School and working full time I would only be there to sleep. I was trying to save up for a car so that I could get around more easily. I didn't have much experience with driving and was nowhere near being ready for my driving test, but these were all on my list of things to accomplish. I had to walk a half mile to the bus stop and then take bus 31 all the way West pass Sawgrass Mall. It was a 45-minute ride and I'd work sometimes until 11pm.

I would encounter the most interesting people on the bus rides. There was a combination of people with mental health issues and hardworking people trying to make a living and go from one place to the next. Anyone boarding the bus with any body odor would have the entire bus stinking with the fumes of their poor hygiene. On my route to work one day the bus was empty. It felt like it was going to be a good bus ride when I boarded. A few stops into the ride a man that was already seated on the bus prior to me boarding came over to sit next to me. I was seated near the window of the two-seater section of the bus. He sat in the aisle seat. People changed seats all the time whenever they were unhappy with their seat for whatever reason, so I didn't find it suspicious at all. He had a very calm demeanor when he spoke to me in Spanish.

"Hola." He didn't speak English. I shook my head to indicate that I did not speak Spanish and continued looking out the window. The man took his right hand and placed it just above my left knee as I was seated. He wasted no time dragging his hand toward my crotch. I pushed his hand away and moved to a different seat. Frustrated, I rang the bell for the bus driver to stop at the upcoming bus stop and got off. I watched the bus pull off and then I cried.

After my fight with Keisha I just focused on working and doing hair. I turned my room at my aunt's place into a salon area with a bed. On my days off from work I'd have clients coming over to get their hair braided.

Months pass before the next time I head from Keisha. She came over to my aunt's house asking me for money to buy her baby some diapers as if our altercation had never happened. I don't hold grudges and I wasn't the one upset so I shook it off and gave her $20. After that we started back hanging out like we had before.

She was no longer dating Kevin, at least not publicly but they were still messing around from time to time. She'd met a new friend, Tyrone, from Dade County. She met him on the chat line just looking for someone to have fun with. Guys from Dade County had way more status than the guys from Broward. For the two counties to be so close, the people were very different and to us, the guys from Dade were just better. They were usually drug dealers, but they had swagger. The boys in Ft. Lauderdale tried to imitate that swag but they just didn't do it right.

She and Tyrone were friends with benefits. They had an understanding that allowed them to have a sexual relationship with no strings attached.

He had a roommate that Keisha described as handsome and charming. She said she wanted me to meet him so we could all hang out together. He had already slept with two of her friends, one with whom he'd dogged out because she wanted to be his girlfriend which violated the agreement. I wasn't at all interested in that. He sounds like a heartbreaker and I was not in any hurry to get my heart broken.

While hanging out at Keisha's one night a dark SUV pulled up in her driveway. It was Tyrone's roommate. Tyron was in the passenger seat. He'd come to see Keisha. A loud smell of marijuana and smoke billowed from the dark tinted windows when he rolled them down to say hello. Anthony invited me to take a walk around the block with him while Keisha and Tyrone handled their business. He was charming for sure, but I knew his reputation and was not about to become the next letter in his alphabet soup of women. Not only was he charming, the conversation was perfect. He had a job and was going to the community college. He liked all the same things that I liked. He was God fearing, loved his mama, and wasn't a thug or a drug dealer. He wanted to focus on school and didn't want a relationship so he had lady friends who would have sex with no strings attached. He was also much older than me. I was about to turn 18 in June, he would be turning 25 in December.

"I can't get in bed with somebody that isn't my man so good luck to you and your *lady friends*." He laughed at my sarcastic tone and I noticed his perfect white teeth. He put his arm around me as we continued to stroll the block talking for hours.

We continued to hang out with Tyrone and Keisha when they'd hook up for sex. We'd have our flirty moments, but I didn't want a friend with benefits, and he didn't want a girlfriend so things between us remained platonic. After some time, he asked me out on a movie date. We went to see the new thriller The Ring at the drive-in. He took me back to his place afterwards and what started as a very bad massage lead to warm kisses on my neck and back. Those warm kisses lead to the first time we made love.

The next day as we were leaving his apartment, we passed another young lady in the hallway beneath the stairs. Anthony was walking behind me, but I could tell the woman was on her way to his apartment. I was not sure if she were visiting Anthony or Tyrone, but she was taken back by seeing him walking with me. I was wearing a denim catsuit that hugged every one of my curves flawlessly. She didn't speak a word as she walked pass, but I saw his reflection in her eyes, and he lowered his head pretending not to know her. She continued up the stairs but stopped before reaching the top and with envious eyes watched us back out of the parking space and pull off in the car. I felt like a winner. He'd chosen me over her. One down, but how many more to go?

We began spending a lot more time together after that. He introduced me to his parents when I rode with him to pick up his laundry from his mom. Anthony would drive all the way from Miami to pick me up from work. I'd go home with him on Friday nights and stay over all weekend. He'd get high and we'd laugh for a good 10 minutes for no reason at all. I guess you could say I was high too. High off love. Anthony was perfect. I was wide open for him. What I admired most was his authenticity. He was real. And he had a good relationship with his mom – just what I'd prayed for.

When one of his close friends announced that he was getting married we had a barbeque at his parents' house while they were out of town to celebrate. I seasoned the meat in the kitchen while Anthony and his friends barbequed out back.

He invited me to spend Christmas with him and his family down in South Miami. Everyone was so friendly and welcoming. I'd purchased some Christmas cards for him to pass out to his friends and family. He asked me to sign them *"From Anthony and Tiffany"* instead of just *"From Anthony"*. His aunt made what she called Fish Tea. A traditional Jamaican seafood soup. My tongue was dancing from all the flavor in the food.

I had no reason to believe that Anthony was being unfaithful to me. Or maybe I didn't notice the signs until the night he received a call from Tahlia. I was listening to music on his phone when the text message popped up. *"I miss you, lol."*

I asked him who's Tahlia and why does she miss him. I maintained a calm tone because I didn't want him to think I didn't trust him, but I had a gut feeling that this was a legitimate concern. He said it was just a friend and she was just joking around hence the LOL in the text. I found it suspicious that there was no other dialogue. The message thread had been deleted so I didn't see and previous conversations between the two. If she were a friend, why are there no previous text messages? No call logs.

I asked him to take me home. I just wasn't buying his story.

Rodney was a long-time loyal client of mine. He stood about 5' 4" and stock with cornrows. He'd always get freestyle braids which meant I'd get to do whatever crazy artistic style I wanted to his hair and he'd always love it. He sold drugs at one point, but he'd taken the drug money and invested it into stocks and bonds and started a business before getting out of the game. He was a protector and provider to his family and the people he loved including me. He never came empty handed and always tipped well. Anyone that he referred to me for braid would do the same. He was one of those clients that had become like family.

Whenever he was on the way to get his hair braided, he'd call and offer to bring me food. This time I wanted fried gizzards and mustard sauce from the seafood restaurant, Pleasures of the Sea.

"I'm not coming from that way today, what else do you want?"

"That's what I want." I snapped. I really had my mind set on tasting Pleasures of the Sea.

"I know but I'm not out that way. I'm by a Wendy's and I'm going to pass a few other places on the way but that's way on the other side of town. "

"You asked me what I want, and I want *Pleasures of the Sea*. If you can't get me that then YOU pick something because that's what I want.

When Rodney arrived, he handed me a double stack meal from Wendy's and a pregnancy test. I laughed at his dramatics. He was adamant that I pee on the stick before I touch his head. To appease him I did what he asked then proceeded to service his cornrows. The service took about 45 minutes and he loved it as usual. I could create the most unique braids in his hair but could never duplicate my work and he loved that. It made him feel exclusive.

After I finished his hair, I went into the restroom to wash my hands. On the sink was the First Response pregnancy test with two pink lines. I asked Rodney to read the box and tell me that didn't mean I was pregnant. It confirmed what he'd already presumed. I was pregnant.

A million thoughts ran through my head in an instant and a slew of emotions. I was shocked, in disbelief, surprised, happy, sad, confused and excited at the same time. Anthony and I hadn't been on speaking terms. The first person I thought to tell was Keisha.

I called her over to my house and with a big smile I showed her the positive pregnancy test. To my surprise she was upset. "I told you to fuck him not fall in love and have a baby from him."

"Excuse me…what makes you think you get to tell me what to do with my body?"

"Tiffany, he doesn't love you. He's not your friend. I'M YOUR FRIEND". She looked like she wanted to cry. Why was she so hurt by this? I know that Anthony and I weren't on speaking terms but that was just a spat. I was probably just overreacting because of the hormones. He was going to be happy and we were going to be happy together.

"You don't know what you're talking about. You're just jealous. You probably wish he wanted to fuck YOU." Why else had she introduced him to two of her other friends before me. I thought about how she spoke so highly of him before I'd even met him. She secretly had a crush on him. Keisha jumped back into her car and sped off in tears. I was crying too. The one person that I thought would be happy for me was angry ad now hurt.

I waited a few hours before calling Anthony to tell him the news. He didn't seem excited, but he didn't seem upset. He was quiet. It was hard to read his thoughts through the phone.

"Am I the only one you've been with?" He asked.

"Of course." I apologized for overreacting about the text message. He just said, "okay" and we ended the call.

I called him back a few days later after scheduling an appointment with a gynecologist. I wanted him to be there. Again, to my surprise he wasn't interested in coming. I could tell that he was agitated but I didn't care. I didn't make the baby by myself and it wasn't fair that he was now being an asshole to me for no reason. A screaming match started between the two of us, but I was silenced by his confession that he he'd just learned that he had another baby on the way. Tahlia was pregnant too. The same Tahlia he'd said was just a friend.

He continued to shout verbal blows of reality in his wrath. "You are not my girlfriend; tiff you were just my favorite. Keisha told me she had this bitch that she needed me to fuck and leave an, so I did. She told me everything I needed to know about you. She told me what to do to get you so I could smash."

Before hanging up the phone he made his proposal, "Do me a favor and have an abortion."

I felt a burning in my chest. I couldn't breathe. My heart was shattered along with my life. I later learned that he'd met Tahlia at the barbeque we held to celebrate his friend's engagement. She was a friend of his friend's girlfriend. His friends all knew about her and even aided him in keeping it from me.

I cried a thousand rivers that night. Not only because my heart was broken. I cried at the thought of raising a baby in such an ugly callous world. I will protect him with my life from anything and anyone who would ever think of hurting him. Reality quickly set in that I wouldn't be able to protect him from everything. I would have to allow life to teach him some hard lessons, that thought was too much for me to take.

I eventually picked up the pieces and accepted the reality that I'd be raising this baby alone. A few bus rides later I'd saved up enough to put a down payment on my first car. Rodney had an auction license and allowed me to join him at a car auction. I purchased my 2002 black Pontiac Sunfire for $800 cash from the auction. It was a stick shift, I had to learn how to drive it. Rodney gave me a few lessons and I caught on quickly.

I enrolled into beauty school to get my braiding license so that I could learn more than just braids and legally do hair in a salon. Into my sixth month of pregnancy I received a call from Anthony. He said that he wanted to be a family and raise our son with me. He invited me to live with him at his mother's house. She wanted to have a relationship with her grandson as well. I hesitated but I remembered my father's words, "Never close the door to the father of your kids. If he wants to be in your life, let him. "So, I did. I accepted the invitation and went to live with Anthony and his parents.

It wasn't long before I realized I'd made a mistake. The phone rang late one night. Anthony answered and I could hear a woman's voice on the other end. When he hung up, I asked, "Who was that?" He sucked his teeth and turned his back to me disregarding my question.

The next morning, I woke up and I took his phone from the nightstand. I went into the restroom and locked the door before I pulled up his call log. It was Tahlia. When he asked me to move in with him, I asked about her and he said it was taken care of. I didn't ask any questions beyond that because he said it was taken care of. I assumed that meant she'd disappeared but apparently, she hadn't. I sent her a test saying not to contact him again.

When he spoke to her and found out what I did he was angry. His friend had come over to chat with him. He stood and watched as Anthony grabbed me by my neck warning me not to ever do that again. That was the first time he got physical with me, but it wouldn't be the last. I got into my car and went back home to my aunt's house.

He called me later that night to apologize and asked me to come back. It didn't sound genuine. It sounded like his mom was pressuring him to smooth things over with me and get me to come back. She and I had formed a tight bond. I'd latched on to her spirit and took her advice when it came to relationships because she had been with her husband since Anthony was two years old. She told me that I needed to grow up. All men cheat and I was going to have to get use to the fact that my man would want to sleep with other women from time to time. She was frank and told me that if I had a problem with that then I wasn't the woman for her son. I received her advice as love and wisdom from a woman who had found the secret recipe for a successful marriage. I just didn't believe that I needed to accept love in this form. It didn't feel like love but what did I know?

Your father and I both had this unrealistic vision of what the perfect relationship would look like. What our perfect "one" would look like. How they'd behave. We both tried to force these characteristics on one another. It was a struggle. Neither of us were completely willing to play the role in each other's dream. We never quite found how to make it work. We remained at odds over time. I held on to the brief moments of happiness and the promise from the elders that things would get better if I'd just hang in there.

My son was born a year and a half after I'd first met his father. Labor was painful and lasted for hours but it was the most beautiful experience. The reward was more. I was alone in the room with the doctors and Anthony's mother, Valencia. I was disappointed that Anthony hadn't made it there to witness the birth of our son. My iron level had dropped significantly. I felt exhausted. I was tired of pushing and begged my doctor to perform a cesarean. As my body grew weary, I remember whispering, "I can't. I can't do this." Abruptly, Anthony entered the room and stood beside me holding my hand. His presence was reassuring. Despite his apprehensions about raising a child. Despite not feeling ready he made it! I couldn't give up now. His presence gave me the strength to push once more. The doctor laid his tiny bloody body on my chest I reached over to feel him with my hands. I counted all 10 fingers and 10 toes. He was perfect. My first example of God's pure and unconditional love.

To my son, I will always do my best as your mother to protect you and I promise you will know love. I apologize if my decision's and my choices in life made it difficult for you to live yours. In the words of Kahlil Gibran, "Out of suffering have emerged the strongest souls; the most massive characters are seared with scars." As you embark on your own journey through life it is my prayer that you never have to suffer the pain of feeling abandoned and ashamed of who you are.

I will teach you humility, to be grateful and to love. And to trust God through every valley experience because he is always by your side when you fall. I pray that your motives are always pure.

In my brokenness, in my regrets, and in my pursuits to love myself and live a spiritually fulfilled and purposeful life - I pray that my choices and mistakes as I navigated through life does not cause you to be confused about yours and doing what is right.

Once I stopped feeling sorry for myself, I realized that even on my darkest nights I was never alone. God always placed someone in my life that, though they weren't seamless, they gave me something to help keep me from falling too far. I had not recognized them as such but over time I learned to recognize and appreciate the little things. It may be a book, or a quote. It could have been a pillow and a bed. I never had to go to bed hungry and I always had a place to lay my head. You have the power to create and recreate your purpose.

CHAPTER 16

"Healing begins where the wound was made."

Alice Walker (The Way Forward is with a broken heart)

*L*oving someone else came more easily to me than loving myself. Though the birth of my son helped me to find the courage to speak up, my journey to elevating myself and healing was a long one. I was immediately overprotective of my son. I read all the baby book like "what to Expect When You're Expecting" and "Caring for Your child, Birth to age 10". The books were helpful in many ways but created anxieties with others. I would not allow anyone to bathe or discipline my son after the things I'd experienced in my past. Not even his father. The books made me suspicious of everything else from daycare abuse to SIDs and the bacteria living all around us. He was born at 32 weeks gestation which was considered premature, but he was otherwise healthy. He never needed any time in the incubator. The doctor said that his immune system was weak, and he would have respiratory issues for years. He would need to be kept away from anyone with as much as a common cold or his reaction could be fatal.

I would still find myself in situations where I'd say, "yes" to something when I really wanted to say, "no". I was confused because there were things that felt wrong but or made me uncomfortable but no one else seemed to be bothered, just me. The exception to that was when it involved my son. I took my role as his protector seriously and was not afraid to lose friends or look bad doing it. People called me crazy. I'd rather they think of me that way. They thought twice before saying anything about my son.

I started working at the bank as a teller when my son was only a month old. Anthony's grandmother was happy to look after him during the day. He was a good baby. Didn't cry much unless he was hungry or needed to be changed. Anthony and I would continue in a toxic, on again off again relationship for another 12 years under the advice of my father.

"Never shut out the father of your kids if he is willing to be there." He'd tell me.

I knew what it was like to have the father absent from the home. The way that it affected me as a little girl. I understood the importance of having balance to the home. I understood how the imbalance could lead to my kids having an unhealthy self-image, low self-esteem, identity conflicts among other things. More than anything in the world I was afraid of having my kids go through what I'd gone through being raised by a stepfather that didn't love them – or worse.

Anthony's mom and I were close before our son was born. His birth drew a ridge between us as she had plans for her grandson that conflicted with who I was as a mother. I WANTED to be active and involved in my son's life. I was open to collaborating with her but not to totally surrender my child to be raised by his grandmother while I go out and live my life as if I had no responsibilities. Where I come from, if you make a baby and don't take care of it, people talk about you. I wanted the full experience of motherhood. The joys as well as the pains. She wanted to take that away from me. She felt threatened by my resistance to do otherwise. Anthony put me out of his mother's house after she told him that I wasn't allowing her to be a part of our son's life. She and I had a disagreement about how many times I should bathe the baby per day. She wanted me to give him a bath every time he had a bowel movement which was several times a day. I expressed concerns about drying out his skin and she suggested using baby oil as a preventative method. He was only weeks old. His pediatrician and all the baby books said that it was best not to bathe the baby so often to avoid dry skin conditions. His sebaceous glands were developing, and we shouldn't interfere with his body's ability to naturally produce oil. She was offended that I placed more value on what the books said rather than trust her knowledge and experience as a mother. I was never impolite in my disagreeing with her, but to her, disagreeing with her WAS disrespectful. Anytime she couldn't get her way with me, she complained to Anthony. He too believed that it was disrespectful to question my elders. He never asked me how I felt. It didn't matter. His mother was offended and that was all he needed to know. I was to do as I was told.

My clashing with Anthony's mother added to our already toxic relationship. Anytime she couldn't get her way with me, she would complain to him and then he and I would fight. My disobedience got me put out of his mom's house when our son was a month old. When his mother learned that the fight had escalated, she told us that we needed to learn how to get along and stop fighting so much. Her attempt to get me to comply had backfired and resulted in him putting me out along with her grandson. That, apparently, wasn't the result she was looking for. I observed how she'd use manipulation to control the people around her. When she couldn't manipulate me, she knew that she could manipulate Anthony. He was accustomed to this as a way of life. It was easier to for him to fight with me and get me to comply rather than respectfully set boundaries for his mother.

"I'm not going to tell my mother how to raise my kid," he said.

My inability to get along with Anthony's mom gave him more reasons to cheat. It justified him in not wanting to come home. The elders in Anthony's family all seems to have family commitment rules like those of my father. I was told that all men cheat and my role was to accept it. My resistance to accepting my role meant I needed to grow up. I was being childish and immature.

Anthony's grandmother told me to pray about it. She straddled both sides of the fence encouraging me to stand up for myself, but she loved her grandson and wanted to see him happy over anything else. She'd experienced a lot of pain and struggle in her life. It made her strong. She spoke her mind without filter.

Anthony's aunt was more of a neutral voice of reason. She was fair in the way she treated everyone. She did not treat me like a child who must do as she was told. She respected me as a woman and as a mother. Instead of forcing her beliefs and criticizing my own, she listened. I never felt invalidated around her which made me more open to trying the new things she presented to me. I trusted her. You never had to question how she felt about something because she was so authentic.

On good days I'd consult with Anthony's mother who'd been married longer than I'd be alive. I wanted to know their secret. I knew that they too had issues with infidelity but if I were to survive in this relationship, I wanted to know what I needed to do to be happy in it. In a heart to heart conversation and with great confidence she enlightened me on her philosophy.

"Men want respect and women want love. The man will not love a woman that does not respect him, and the woman will not respect a man that does not love her. You need to respect your man enough to let your man do what he wants to do. Give him space, he will come around." She shared with me that she'd just paid for her husband's flight to New York where he was going to visit another woman. He of course told her that he was going for another reason, but she knew the truth. She remined silent. With an assertive tone she said, "And when my husband gets home, I'm going to have his dinner ready because *this* is his castle and I AM his queen."

"Your man is going to want to see other women from time to time. It doesn't make you any less his woman, it doesn't make him any less of a man. If you are not okay with that, then you are not the woman for my son."

At church, the Pastor said, "You'll know when you've made the right decisions because you'll feel peace in your heart." In other sermons he'd also speak against divorce and give constant reminders to stand strong.

I listened to all of it growing more and more confused. I went along with life accepting it as just that, life. Letting it happen and relinquishing my control over what happens and how it happens. I was no to be trusted with this power just yet. I had no idea what to do with it. It was some time before I realized that many of these people were feeding me the same lies, they'd told themselves. While I do believe they all thought they were giving me the best advice and doing so in love. Many of them were giving me advice rooted in their own misery. We all know how much misery loves company.

Our son was two and a half years old when we gave birth to our second child. A beautiful little girl. Before that night our son had never slept overnight with anyone other than me or his dad. He stayed over with my dad. As soon as I gave birth to my daughter, I called my dad to bring him to the hospital where he slept next to me in the hospital bed until I was discharged to go home.

After giving birth to our second child, despite promises of change from the elders in his family, there was more of the same. They were convinced that the birth of his daughter would be the pivot point for him, and he would change. At my 6-week check-up I tested positive for chlamydia and BV. I was devastated. My gynecologist had performed routine STD tests back in December. Our daughter was born late in April. My 6-week post-partum visit was in June. That mean he'd slept with someone else unprotected within those six months.

When I confronted him about the test results, he put on an Oscar winning performance. He was just as shocked as I was.

"How did you get that?" He asked. "Who you been with." This was not only an insult to my intelligence but also an insult to my morals and values. I'd never shared my body with another man since we started. Despite being on again – off again, I had no desire to defile my body. He was the only person I'd been with. During our off period I'd focus on healing. I was happiest when we weren't together but still felt a soul tie that wouldn't wash off in the shower.

After hours of lying and denying he finally confessed that he'd slept with a woman he'd met at work. I immediately knew it was the one that he was talking to on the phone one night while hidden in our son's room in the dark. I had heard him speaking softly to someone late one night, but I never said anything. When he went to sleep, I'd checked his call log and saw "Jessica and sis". Jessica was one of the kids he worked with, "Sis" was the hoe that he slept with.

"She came to pick up her sister often and we'd flirt but nothing happened." He said it all started as harmless flirting. "She's getting married and said she just wanted to fuck me one time before she tied the knot. It only happened once; I swear" That was his story.

After that I couldn't stand his touch. It felt like I was lying down next to a poisonous snake. Sex with him wasn't always pleasureful. Most of the time it was "wam bam thank you ma'am" and then he goes outside to smoke. There was no affection, no foreplay and I was bored with the same two positions. Missionary style and doggy style. Any request or suggestion of any "spicing up" of our sex life always resulted in accusations that I was seeing someone else – or that I wanted to. He said he wanted me to stay wholesome. I never experienced an orgasm with him, but I'd never rejected his sexual advances before out of loyal and fear that "what I won't do, another woman will." It bothered me to know that he was having unprotected sex with other women. This one – according to him- was a onetime thing and still he didn't value his life enough to wear a condom. If he doesn't value his own life, he surely doesn't value mine. I thought there were rules to this thing. How am I expected to "submit" myself to this?

I began having nightmares about him cheating. In one dream I walked into our bedroom to find a Latina on top of him in our bed. She was prettier than me, skinnier than me and sexier than me. He was busy enjoying the ride and didn't notice I was standing there in the doorway watching them work. But she noticed. She looked up and locked eyes with me while stroking my man right in front of me. He was moaning and she was smiling up at me with a devilish grin.

I started working out with a personal trainer mostly because I was having a hard time bouncing back after having the baby. It had only been two months, but I thought because I had gained that extra weight from the pregnancy, I wasn't sexy enough. It started out that way, but I became addicted to how I felt after my workouts. I became obsessed with healthier living and taking better care of my body, mind, and spirit. Anthony was not at all happy with the amount of time I was spending with my male personal trainer. I was working out 6 days a week and the results started to show rather quickly. My trainer and I did become very close friends, but the relationship was strictly platonic. He was never inappropriate with me. He challenged me and encouraged me to be the best version of myself and cheered for me which is something no one had done for me in years. I hadn't even done it for myself. I felt balanced.

The birth of our daughter in conjunction with the STD gave me more confirmation that nothing was going to change – still I stayed. Our relationship was unhealthy. I asked him to leave and he did. When he tried coming back, I'd changed the locks. A week or two later I'd be giving him the key.

He wouldn't want anything to do with the kids if we weren't together. He knew this would bother me because I never wanted my kids to be fatherless. It was usually the kids that would be the reason we'd speak again. My little girl wouldn't stop crying one night after he'd left. I couldn't figure out what was wrong with her. She was running a fever but no other symptoms. I thought maybe she was gassy, nothing helped. She was crying relentlessly for over an hour when I called Anthony and asked him to come get our son so that I could take her to the emergency room. The moment he walked in the door and picked her up she stopped crying.

What the hell?

"She missed her daddy that's all." Anthony was convinced that she was suffering from nothing more than a broken heart. I, myself, was convinced. Had I not witnessed her performance myself I would not have believed it. She fell asleep in his arms and the fever broke. I connected with the love she felt for him. It was how I felt about my daddy. I don't recall ever having such strong separation anxieties for him, but I craved having him around.

I told my father I wasn't happy. I begged him to let me come home. He came and picked me up after one of our fights got physical. He didn't ask what happened, he wasn't interested in the details and I wasn't interested in telling them. The next morning, he woke me up and told me it was time to go home and talk things out with my man. I was upset but I knew that people had grown to see the pattern of our relationship. I always took him back within a week or two. Sometimes less. We'd break up, he'd take away the keys to the car leaving me to call on other people or take a cab to get the kids to daycare and myself to work. I wasn't fooling anyone but myself.

Anthony joined me at my follow up visit with my gynecologist. This is where he chose to propose to me. In the clinic. While getting tested for STDs.

"We should get married." He whispered in the crowded waiting area of the doctor's office. There was no ring, no dropping on one knee, no fireworks. This was not how this was supposed to be happening. I thought he can't be serious. He was.

"My answer will be contingent upon the results of this lab work."

I recommended that we get premarital counseling at my church.

We were sitting in a premarital session with my Pastor when things became clear to me that we were making a mistake. The pastor read scriptures to reference the role of the husband, the role of the wife and the significance of this covenant with God. He asked a list of questions about our relationship. Are you happy with your sex life? Do you feel safe talking to your significant other about anything? I wanted to answer these questions honestly, but Anthony just wanted to give the right answer whether it was truth or not. We'd have an argument right there in front of the pastor because he was lying. I was uncomfortable with lying in this setting. Anthony disagreed; he was telling what he referred to as "his truth".

"It can't be anyone's truth if it's a LIE."

I was NOT free to speak my mind and share my thoughts. I was NOT happy with our sex life. I did NOT feel safe speaking openly and honestly about how I felt. I did NOT trust Anthony's ability to lead our family.

My Pastor asked to meet with us separately. He began my session by reading the frequently quoted 1st Corinthians. I remembered a short story I'd read where marriage counselors would recommend replacing the word, "Love" with that of the person you believe is love. I made mental checkmarks to help me to further determine if this was indeed love.

"Love is patient, Love is kind." Anthony is patient, Anthony is kind. Negative. He had very little patience for me and didn't value much of anything I had to say. Kind? He was kind to other people but not to me. I felt like he hated me. He felt trapped in this situation and like me, he was just doing what people expected us to do which was get married.

"Love does not envy." I couldn't recall him every being envious of me. He believed that he deserved better. I wasn't enough for him. I did, however recall that he would shut down any ideas I had of going to college or doing something to elevate myself.

"It does not boast; it is not proud." Anthony wasn't very boastful. Not with me. I knew things that he preferred to keep hidden from the world. He was more concerned with his image in the way that *other* people viewed him. My job was to maintain that image. When I moved in to my first apartment, we were on one of our "off" periods. He was still living with his mom and making frequent visits to the other women. He helped me move in and never left. He contributed nothing towards 1st month, last month's rent and the deposits required to move in nor the utilities. He didn't help pay any of the bills. He said he wanted to focus on paying off his IRS debt and his truck so that we could buy a house. He invested $200 from each paycheck toward his family's pot. The rest of his money went on hoes, clothes, and weed.

"it is not rude; it is not self-seeking." Who are we talking about?

"it is not easily angered." Ha!

"it keeps no record of wrongs" This is sad. It's not looking at all like love to me.

"Love does not delight in evil but rejoices in the truth." Yet here we are lying to the pastor.

"It always protects, always trusts, always hopes, always perseveres, Love never fails." At this point, just throw me in the garbage because I feel like trash. I felt convicted of not knowing love and not allowing myself to receive the love that God promised me. What does love to look like? It was written right there in His word. Nothing confusing about that. God wanted better for me, but I was running towards the very things he was trying to shield me away from.

My Pastor asked me, why are you with him? I had no words. I was stuck.

Now that I know better, I'd have to do better. I told Anthony I didn't think we were ready for marriage. He did not take the rejection well and it created more of a rift in our relationship. This would be our longest separation period.

This time things would be different. I knew that I wanted things to change but I had no idea how to change them. Leaving that relationship was a start but how could I be sure that I wouldn't take him back in another moment of weakness? I needed to DO something different. Something I'd never done before. Something that would guarantee that things would never be the same. I'd move on with my body.

I met Larry in traffic one morning on my way to workout at the park. The first thing I noticed was his smile. It was contagious. We were both stopped at the traffic light when he signaled for me to roll down my window.

"What's your name?" he shouted across the lane and his empty passenger seat. I had a mouth full of apple I hadn't finished chewing. I covered my mouth and tried not to laugh and spit out my apple. I held up my index finger with my other hand.

The light turned green. Before pulling off he motioned for me to follow him to the park across the street. He pulled over into the park and I followed. I stayed inside my car, but he got out and came over to talk to me.

"It's Tiffany." I had finished my apple.

"I'm Larry, you're beautiful." I thanked him for the compliment before he went on to ask me if he could take me to dinner. I didn't find him attractive, but he seemed nice, so I accepted. He was on his way to work; I was on my way to my trainer's Saturday Full Body bootcamp. After a moment of friendly flirting we exchanged telephone numbers and went on our way.

Anthony and I were on the last leg of our relationship when I'd met

Larry. I only toyed with the idea of seeing someone else. Larry became attached to me sharing his fears and past traumas. He was grieving the loss of his child from years before. The loss of his child ultimately leads to the dissolution of his marriage. He was still healing. I knew that Larry had developed strong feelings for me over time. He knew that I was in a broken relationship and often suggested that I leave Anthony to be with him. He offered lavish gifts and invited me on romantic trips with him. Each time I refused he would get discouraged but it didn't stop him from trying again. I wanted our relationship to remain platonic. I wasn't interested in being with him romantically. The thought of leaving something familiar for the unfamiliar was scary enough. That in conjunction with my fear of having my kids raised by a man other than their father left me mortified. Despite his promises to give me the world and treat me the way I deserved to be treated, I just couldn't.

My feelings changed just a bit now that Anthony and I were over, and I'd decided to try something new. Larry would be the perfect rebound guy. I felt comfortable enough to be romantic with him but not enough to get emotionally involved. I just wanted the sex. I needed to prove to myself that I was my own woman, possessed by no man.

I initiated the hook up. I was the aggressor. I was in control.

We had dinner at Hibachi Grill before meeting up at his apartment. My youngest sister had come for an extended visit with me and helped with the kids. He had prepared his space to a most romantic greeting. Candles lined the hallway leading to his bedroom. On the floor of the bedroom, rose peddles formed a heart with the letters T and L in the middle. Champagne was chilling in a metal container full of ice. Why couldn't Anthony be this romantic? In the years we'd been together we only celebrated Valentine's day if I funded it. The same thing for my birthday and any family vacations.

I didn't expect romance tonight. I just expected sex. He, however, had other things in mind.

I enjoyed being romanced. It was something I never experienced in my relationship. Only in the fantasies of my mind. His kisses were sloppy and wet. I felt like I was being attacked by a happy go lucky mastiff. I needed to shut that down quickly before it kills the mood entirely. It wasn't easy but I managed to minimize kisses that night. I'd turn my head offering my neck as his chew toy among other things. He traveled south slowly exploring my body with his tongue. My knees started get weak and trembled. He picked me up. My legs secured on his shoulders and wrapped around his neck. His tongue never stopped maneuvering between my legs like he was drinking the last of the soup from the pot. He walked over to the wall and lowered me slowly from his face to his waist where he entered me. The end. After a few strokes I heard him growl then it was over. I wasn't entirely disappointed with his size. It wasn't impressive but I could work with it. I prefer an average sized penis over an elephant dick anyway. I didn't find pleasure in the pain of having my insides beaten up and swollen. That type of sex was more pain than pleasure.

He'd climaxed so quickly. I was hoping for something more so when he went into the shower, I grabbed another condom and joined him for round two. His wet kisses were filtered by the warm water running from the shower head. Still I offered other parts of my body for him to kiss. I stroked his penis with my hand until he was ready. Round two was wet and steamy but we were both uncomfortable. He wasn't as confident when he picked me up in the shower. I wasn't at all excited at the idea of him dropping me.

We exited the bathroom and went over to the bed to finish off the second round. He bent me over and kept his hands on my waist. This was a bad idea. He struggled to resist the climax, stopping to pull out after several strokes whenever he felt the loss of control. This was exasperating. I'm ready to wrap it up. Moments later he was growling again, and it was over. I just rolled up under the covers and went to sleep unsatisfied. Sometime during the night, I woke up to use the restroom. I noticed semen on the tissue that I used to wipe myself. He had to have ejaculated inside of me for that to happen, but how? When? I watched him put on a condom each time. While the risk of sexually transmitted disease was a concern, I wasn't on any birth control. This wasn't fun anymore.

I woke him up in a panic. "Larry where is the condom from last night?"

"Huh?" He responded in a daze. His brain was taking too long to wake up.

"Where is the condom? There's semen inside of me." I was getting annoyed. Why wasn't he freaking out?

"I think it broke." He mumbled with his eyes still closed.

"It BROKE??? WHEN? Why didn't you tell me? What do you mean you THINK it broke? Did it break or not?" I was franticly searching the garbage for the condom hoping he hadn't flushed it. "Where did you put it?"

From the corner of my eye I noticed the off-white balloon like material on the floor near the base on the bed. I examined the condom. It wasn't broken. Yet there was no semen inside.

I began convulsing. I was having a panic attack. It was hard for me to make sense of what was happening in that moment. "Larry what did you do?" I asked. Holding back tears. He said he thought the condom broke, so he took it off. It didn't make any sense to me why he would take off the condom and not put on another one even if he did think it was broken. And why would you ejaculate inside of me? Why didn't you pull out knowing you had done that?" We were both wet from our brief intermission in the shower. I hadn't noticed the difference.

I felt so stupid; this was all a big mistake. The dinner, the sex, all of it. I should have never come here. I believed this was God punishing me for defiling my body. As I'd come to be more active and involved in ministry, I knew that God would not be pleased with my actions and this was the consequence. It was around 4am when I decided to leave. I asked Larry to meet me at the pharmacy to purchase a Plan B pill since this was all his fault. He agreed.

I couldn't sleep at all when I got home. The pharmacy near me apartment opened at 7am. I would be there at 6:45. I called Larry's phone, but he didn't answer. I left a message, sent a text, and a DM to his Facebook account before I'd get a response.

"I have to go open up at work and let the staff in and then I'll be right there." He said. I waited an hour, but he never came. I called again. He was still at the office.

I was furious that he was being so nonchalant about this. I didn't want any more kids. Two was plenty. If I was to have another one it would ONLY be from a man that is my husband. I didn't want to be anyone's baby mama. Having a 3rd child from a man that is not my husband was not in the stars.

"Relax." He commanded. "It's a certain kind of cum that you can get pregnant from and that isn't it." You won't get pregnant. This was the craziest thing I've ever heard a man say. What kind of semen was it? Chocolate semen? Minty fresh?

He never did show up to the pharmacy. I pleaded with him and waited for hours until I finally just purchased it myself. There were two pills in the package. The instructions were to take the first one immediately and take the second pill 12 hours later. In my rage I left a long voicemail for Larry full of "fuck yous" and attacks on his integrity. I strongly believed that he removed the condom intentionally in hopes of getting me pregnant. I knew that he desperately wanted a child, but I never imagined he would go to such lengths to make one…and with me.

This experience was a wakeup call for many things. I was behaving in a manner that was opposite of who I was. Again, placing myself in a situation that I wasn't prepared to handle. I thought doing this would help me to move forward but I was going backwards. I prayed and asked God to forgive me for this sin against my body and promised to never do this again. I would honor my body just as the scriptures command.

After a couple of weeks Anthony started to come around again asking if he could come home. He was offering to help around the house and interacting with the kids. Doing laundry, and dishes - everything that he knew would get him back into good graces with me. It worked a little. I enjoy having the much-needed help. My sister had stayed only a week, but she left to visit a friend and never came back. I think she was starving from all the healthy food I had in my house. She sat around all day eating breakfast cereal which was the closest thing I had to junk food. Everything else was healthy low-calorie food.

I knew that Anthony and I weren't healthy for each other. I loved the way our kids loved him. To my kids, I knew that having him around was priceless even if that meant sacrificing my own happiness. To me his presence in their lives was what was most important. I allowed him to come over as often as he liked, even staying overnight, but he had to sleep in the room with the kids. He didn't refute my request.

Weeks later I was at work having lady talk. After working in banking for 7 year and growing in the field, a recession would cause the bank to merge with a bigger corporation. Everyone in the operations department was offered positions in other departments. I'd worked my way up from teller to teller supervisor, then a customer service supervisor, before being promoted to Operations. I was not willing to go to the collections department. The pay was commission based on what was recovered. There was a high earning potential, but you had to be willing to be a shark. That meant calling neighbors and friends to recover funds from someone who can't afford to pay their mortgage, or loans. I saw this as an opportunity to go into business for myself. I was going to school and living off student loans and my savings when my son's godmother asked me to work with her at her therapy clinic as the office manager. We were discussing how our menstrual cycles had synchronized as well as our moods. She and I were always on our period at the same time, but her period had just ended a few days before. That was the exact moment when we both realized I hadn't gotten my period this month. She read my thoughts without my having to say anything.

"Maybe you're just stressed out or changing cycles." She saw the anxiety on my face and tried to calm n nerves. A pregnancy test I purchased at the pharmacy would prove otherwise. My worse fear had become my reality. I was pregnant again.

I cried my eyes out that night. I had committed the sin of adultery and was now contemplating murder by abortion. Maybe it's not his baby. Maybe I was already pregnant before I slept with him. I decided the right thing to do would be to own my mistake and deal with the consequences of my choices. Anthony smiled when I showed him the pregnancy test. His smile disappeared when he saw my tears.

"There's someone else." I confessed. I told Anthony everything. I'd never seen him cry this hard before. I expected rage. He'd shake me, choke me, beat me up. Something other than cry. The new of me sharing my body with another man had hurt him deeply. The way I felt watching him cry like that made me wish he would've hit me instead. He slept in my bed that night. We didn't do much talking at all. There was just the silence and tears shared between the two of us. He turned over so that his back was no longer to me in bed and lifted my head pulled my face closer to his. In my shame I avoided direct eye contact. I couldn't stand to look at myself. I felt dirty. I was both confused and relieved when he leaned in closer and gave me passionate kiss.

"It's going to be okay." He whispered. I began to cry again. He held me tightly and told me he wasn't going anywhere. "We can raise the baby together no matter what the results are. No one must know there was ever anyone else.

CHAPTER 17

*A*nthony joined me at the Women's Center the next day. Here they would be able to tell me just how far along I was. Knowing the date of conception would help us to determine if the baby was his or not. If it wasn't his baby, we could decide whether to terminate the pregnancy right away or keep it.

The conception date was determined by ultrasound which was a more accurate method than the date of the last menstrual period. I was 6 weeks and three days pregnant. The results proved that it was not Anthony's baby. Before last night, we had not had sex since he'd started coming back around. The date of conception was after we'd already broken up. He was hopeful that the baby would be proven to be his. The news of the contrary was a double dagger to his heart. He didn't say anything when the doctor was sharing the result with us and giving us our options. It was impossible for me to read him. I told the doctor we'd discuss it in private and I'd contact the office if I decided to terminate.

The silence continued as we exited the office and entered our SUV to drive home. He then broke his silence, shouting out in pain and punched the stirring wheel. I tried to embrace him, but he pushed my arm away and exited the vehicle. He went to take a walk. I gave him his space.

He came back to join me in the car. He was breathing fast and had obviously been crying again. He kissed me. "It's okay. I deserve it."

I was shocked at his words. He was blaming himself and his past transgressions for my behavior. I was seeing a different side of him. He was holding himself accountable for his contributions to the path our relationship took. I felt tremendous guilt and shame. The actions were my own. I didn't blame him, but he was blaming himself. He was even willing to forgive me and keep the baby knowing it wasn't his.

Over the next few weeks the situation began to eat away at his pride and his ego. We discussed whether I should tell Larry that I was pregnant and allow him to decide if he wanted to be a part of the baby's life of not. Anthony was not at all happy with that idea, but I wanted to do the right thing. It felt wrong to do otherwise. What if he or she grows up with this lie and identity issues and resents us for it. I wanted to at least be able to tell our child that we tried to allow his biological father to be there. Anthony was against this for multiple reasons, mostly rooted in pride and insecurities.

Against his wishes I did contact Larry again. He didn't answer my call. I don't blame him, the last words I spoke to him were very mean and harsh. I left him a voicemail message asking him to call me and informing him that I was pregnant. He did not return my call and that was the end of that. My conscience was clean. I tried.

Anthony was upset that I contacted Larry behind his back. He thought that my contacting him meant that I had some feelings for him. Over time he got more and more paranoid and suspicious about the truth behind our relationship. The severity of the damage caused started to surface more and more after that. I would later learn that he'd researched Larry on social media. He'd finally put a face with the name. He had his phone number, tag number, home address another personal information. He knew his birthday and the type of car he drives. We would be in traffic, having casual lighthearted conversation and his mood would totally change at the sight of a silver mustang. September 12th, the date of conception, would forever be a sad day for him.

We started arguing more frequently. The arguments would escalate until he was storming out again disappearing for a day or two. After an awkward thanksgiving dinner with his family, everyone was congratulating us on the pregnancy which was evident at this point. It wasn't a secret anymore. I decided to take the kids and drive up to Orlando for the weekend just to get away. My uncle lived in Orlando and had been inviting us to come up and stay at his place for a few days. It was a 3 hour long drive I'd take alone with my 2 kids in the car. They slept most of the way. When we arrived and greeted my uncle and his wife, we got unpacked and went out to explore the city. There was a Winter Wonderland Festival of lights, a carnival with ice and rides recreating what you'd expect to see in a northern state that seasonally experienced snow in autumn. In Florida, the temperatures in autumn would range anywhere from cool to hell. They'd created a replica of icy hills where the kids could go snowboarding and sledding.

My son woke up that night with a fever. "Mommy I see everything two times." This boy would get sick every time the wind changed directions. He'd been treated for asthma, scarlet fever, influenza, strep throat, and bronchial infections among other things. The doctor had warned that although he was born healthy, his premature birth would mean that his respiratory system had not fully developed in the womb and he'd have some issues.

I could handle a fever. I knew to look out for other symptoms before taking him to the emergency room. Double vision was a symptom I had not yet experienced. I took him to a hospital in Orlando where they diagnosed him with pneumonia. We'd be spending the next few days in the hospital by his side. Anthony took a flight from Fort Lauderdale to Orlando to join us. He put on a smile whenever my uncle or the doctors were around but when we were alone the mask came off. It was most unpleasant being stuck in the hospital room with him being all miserable and making derogatory comments about me under his breath. I ignored the personal jabs he was taking. He obviously wanted attention, but this was not the time nor the place.

I smiled too big while talking the doctor when he was discharging our son. "Why don't you let doc hit it too?" He asked. He chuckled at what he thought was a clever joke. I ignored him and decided not to give him the reaction he was looking for, so did the doctor.

"Thank you, Doctor." I shook the doctor's hand and we made our exit. We went back to my uncle's house only to retrieve our belongings before getting back on the road to head home. It was quiet for the first hour of the drive. Anthony was being childish playing music like "Fuck What I Said" by Eamon. Songs that contained lyrics he could use to taunt me. When I wouldn't react, he became more animated singing so loudly that not even the kids could get any sleep. I participated by singing along.

The song said, "Fuck you, you hoe. I don't want you back." I changed the lyrics and said, "Fuck you too, hoe. I don't want you back." He was enjoying our sing along a little too much. Purposefully changing the words to any song so that he could call me a bitch or a hoe. When I was ready to stop playing along, he wanted to continue. I turned down the music and asked him to stop.

"Nah, bitch lets sing about it." He was smiling. He turned up the volume and continued to sing loudly.

"Anthony, stop. The kids are right there watching us and listening. It's gone far enough." He continued despite my request to stop. "If you have something you want to say to me just say it Anthony but I'm not about to sit her and let you verbally abuse me for 3 hours."

"Fuck you, bitch." He was still singing.

"I'm serious. I will pull this car over and you can call somebody else to come and get you." I gave no immediate response to my threat but continued to play explicit music in the car.

"You fucked my friend and then threaten to put me out of the car?" He was talking to me, and his words were directed toward me, but I never slept with any of his friends, so I had no idea what he was talking about. But he was ready to talk so I let him vent. "Me and your boy work together."

In his digging for information about Larry, Anthony had learned that he and Larry's employers had caused them to cross paths. They were both in a conference together in the past. They'd met during the conference they had lunch together. That was the extent of the relationship. I had no idea. Larry had never mentioned knowing or knowing of Anthony at all. I don't even think he remembered. Anthony didn't even remember. Here he was sulking and carrying on like I'd slept with his friend and believing this justified him speaking harshly to me and behaving this way.

"I can't believe this man fucked my girl like that?"

"You sound so stupid. That's not your friend. He doesn't even know you." I was annoyed that this was the reason he'd been acting like an ass."

"Did you like it?" He asked.

"What?"

"The sex. Did you like it?"

"I'm not going to answer that question." I refused to answer the question because I Believe that no matter what my answer was it was going to be the wrong answer period if I said I did enjoy it he would get upset. If I said I did not enjoy it, he would think that I'm only saying that to appease him. Either way it was a lose-lose. My refusal to engage and that questioning made him even more upset. The arguing erupted yet again. He went back to shouting insults and calling me names.

I got off at the next exit and pulled into the nearest gas station where I told him to get out.

"Get out of my car." I ordered.

"You really gonna put me out on the side of the road?"

"It's a gas station. Figure out where you're at and call somebody else to come get you." I was over it. We were about an hour away from home. Arguing for so long was draining the life out of me. The situation had taken a toll on him. I was willing to terminate the pregnancy as soon as we learned it wasn't his. He wanted to keep it. He thought he could handle it but clearly, he had been damaged significantly. It had created insecurities that lead to him hating this man and resenting me. Larry had moved on with his life and had no idea how much this man wanted his head on a stick. I had no idea what Anthony was capable of at this point. He was unpredictable, behaving irrationally. What would happen if they ever crossed paths again? Larry would be blindsided. This was all my fault. I needed to fix the mess I'd made. I was right. Moving no with my body was the perfect way to ensure that Anthony and I would never be the same.

The next day my ex-coworker, Shauna, whom I now call friend, accompanied me to the clinic to terminate my pregnancy. The atmosphere in the back felt totally different from the front office where I'd received my ultrasound. The back room was quiet. No one was happy to be there. Death and sadness could be felt in the air. There was an assembly line of girls in hospital gowns along the wall. One by one they called the girls in. They would not come out the same way. They'd be escorted by foot into the recovery room by two assistants holding them up. They'd be barely standing. When it was my turn I walked into the room. There was a hospital bed surrounded by medical tools and a blank white wall with bright lights in the ceiling. The doctor was wearing a light blue mask over his mouth and a blue medical cap on his head. He was washing his hands before putting on gloves. The medical assistants wasted no time strapping me down to the bed and prepping me for the procedure. They didn't care about your feelings. They weren't gentle or kind. They made no effort to make the patient feel more at ease about the process or their decision. And it was too late to turn back. I was 16 weeks pregnant.

"You're going to feel warm." The doctor warned as he injected a clear liquid into my arm. It didn't feel warm it felt hot. I felt like the blood in my body was on fire and it was running through my veins.

I cried out to the doctor, "It burns." He proceeded to open my legs despite my cry. "No. Please stops. It burns." My entire body went numb. I felt a tear fall from my eyes, but I couldn't move. I felt pressure and then pain when the doctor performed the procedure to break apart my unborn baby. I heard what sounded like a vacuum, but I couldn't move my neck to see what was happening.

I was still crying, "It hurts. I can feel it. It hurts." But he couldn't stop. He finished the procedure and the assistants lifted me up to a standing position so that they can help me put my underwear on. I still had no control over my body. I passed out.

When I came to. I was in the recovery room. Shauna, by my side. She was holding my hand. She knew how hard of a decision this was for me, but she had no idea how torturous the entire experience was. It was the equivalent of being strapped down and violently raped.

Shauna took me to get some food from a Jamaican restaurant on the way home. I couldn't eat. I balled up on the couch in the dark and cried myself to sleep. The guilt of what I'd just done to my baby and the actions that lead to it would haunt me for years. Every time I looked into the eyes of a baby; it'd feel like that baby saw my sin. I felt the pain of my baby in those babies' eyes and I'd apologize. Over and over I was sorry.

We told everyone I'd miscarried. When people asked what happened, I responded with I don't want to talk about it. That was the God honest truth. I didn't want to talk about it at all. Anthony continued living with his parents and visiting frequently to spend time with the kids. He was back to sleeping in their room with them and they loved it.

After my experience at the abortion clinic I wasn't at all interested in having him or anyone else touch me. I didn't want anything inserted into my vagina. For months I would refuse his sexual advances. He never handled the rejection well but since he now knew that I could have sex with someone other than him he was taking my rejection more personally. He assumed it meant I was involved with someone else. I wasn't. I was still healing physically, emotionally, and psychologically. I'd made a mistake and was having a hard time forgiving myself. That mistake came with an abundance of lessons about life and consequences that I'd have to live with forever.

I channeled my focus into building my salon business and my relationship with God. My pastor encouraged me to get active in ministry. He recommended the First Friends Ministry. The ministry welcomed new member to the church and -for some- to Christ. It was a big responsibility because we were touching many souls that were struggling spiritually. It's easy to feel insignificant in a big church. We wanted everyone to know that they were important to the church body. Some were lost, some were just looking for a new church home. Our job was to help these new disciples get acclimated to their new church family through prayer, counseling, and offer resources. Whatever they needed. This ministry wasn't for just anyone. It requires a significant amount patience. You had to be friendly, personable and spiritually grounded. So many of the people I encountered were hurting. They would call my phone late at night for prayer and I had to respond. I didn't know how to pray for other people.

I was uncomfortable praying out loud. I had to be obedient to the spirit. God was the reason I was still alive.

When my pastor recommended that I join this ministry out of all the other available ministries I was reluctant at first. I, myself, was still growing spiritually. I still had times when I doubted God. I still doubted myself.

"You're perfectly imperfect." He said to me.

I did not realize the profound impact the ministry would have on me. The other servants in the ministry shared the same heart to want to help others heal but had experienced brokenness of their own. The ministry became my family. We would meet up outside of church and fellowship together building relationships. We represented the family of Christ and had to be examples of His love. Through them I learned to embrace who I am. Flaws and all. In my brokenness, I was given the opportunity to help others heal. To be the light that I had seen so very little of in the world. To be a vessel for God.

The relationships that were built through the ministry helped me to elevate spiritually. If ever I'd miss a Sunday service, my energy would be thrown off for the entire week.

Back home I was still going through hell, but I'd learned to embrace the lessons within. Months had passed and I was nowhere closer to wanting to be intimate with Anthony. We were still living apart and I knew that he had been involved sexually with other women. I'd loss all sexual desire not only for him but for anyone. He resorted to what was familiar to him which was aggressive force. He tried to force his way into my bedroom one night, but my door was locked. The next morning, he picked a fight hoping that the fight would lead to makeup sex. He couldn't comprehend that I was not responding to his sexual advances for any reason other than I simply was not interested. He was convinced I'd been involved with another man.

After an exchange of words, I asked him to leave. He refused. He went into the bathroom to shower and I turned off the water. "No, you need to leave, now. Go shower at your mama's house. Why are you over here bothering me anyway? Go harass one of your hoes. Let one of them hoes give you some ass"

"I am!" He said.

"Me too." He was so hell bent on believing that I was sleeping with someone else I thought I'd just tell him what he wanted to hear so that he would leave me alone. What happened was the opposite. He took down the entire shower curtain trying to grab me. I ran toward the kitchen hoping to find something I could use to defend myself. I didn't know he could run so fast. He grabbed me and picked me up by my neck. I could feel his other hand tightly gripping my side. He was covered in soap. I couldn't get a good grip onto any part of his body. He threw me onto the bed and climbed on top of me placing a euro pillow over my face. I was struggling to breathe, and he was pressing down hard.

Our son must've heard the commotion and came to investigate. I'm not sure how long he'd been standing in the doorway when I heard him shout out to his dad.

"Daddy what are you doing to mommy?"

"Nothing babe. We were just playing." He immediately released his grip and I was able to breathe. I pushed him off me. He laughed and hit me with the pillow to convince our son that we were indeed playing a game.

He got dressed, kissed the kids and left my apartment as if nothing had happened. I shared what happened with a friend who called the police. The police came to my apartment and questioned me about what happened. Anthony was arrested later that day on a battery charge and spent the night in jail before being bailed out.

"You should never call the police on your man no matter what he does. Never let the police into your home." His mother and other member of his family were upset that I'd violated one of the many laws of how to survive in a dysfunctional relationship. As a result of my actions, the father of my kids could lose his job or go to prison or both. This was my fault. I should not have said what I said. I should learn to keep my tongue.

In my other ear was my friends telling me that I wasn't wrong. He had no right to put his hands on me and deserved whatever happened to him as a result of his actions. My church friends rallied around me offering food and assistance with the kids for a few days. This all happened the week of Thanksgiving. We had Thanksgiving dinner with member of our church family and leftovers to get us through the week.

The restraining order prevented Anthony from speaking to me or coming near me or our kids until our court date which was months away. He had a birthday coming up. I felt bad that he hadn't been able to see the kids. They were asking to see him. On his birthday I drove out to his office building and parked across the street from his job. He'd spotted my car and stood with his hands folded across his chest. The kids were blindfolded. They had no idea where we were going. I didn't want them telling anyone and risk getting him into any more trouble – he was visibly defensive.

I took the kids out of the car one and then took off their blindfolds facing away from their dad. Then I turned them around and they saw him. It wasn't a busy street at all. I walked them to the edge of the street and then released them to run to him. They embraced him with big hugs. He lowered his guard realizing I came in peace. Still I kept my distance. Without saying a word, I walked back over to my car to allow him his moment. I waited for his signal that he was done spending time with the kids.

When it was time to go to court, I couldn't go through with it. Giving a testimony that I knew would result in jail time or him losing his job was the hardest thing for me to do. I'd been told that if I didn't cooperate my kids could be taken away from me. Once I learned that this wasn't true for my case I no longer cooperated. The case was dropped.

My dad had his first heart attack at age 50. His failing organs were a result of his sickle cell anemia. He further complicated things with his past drug use and poor eating habits. He had been in the hospital a few days before I found out he had been there. My dad never wanted his kids to know when he was hurting. He didn't want to burden us. He was also stubborn and didn't want to appear weak. I guess that where I get it from. One of the reasons I'd never like to share details of my relationship problems with my father was because I never wanted to disappoint him or burden him with my troubles on top of his own. I wanted to make him proud and I wanted him to be happy. We always knew that his time would not be long. His sickle cell disease was taking its toll. His body was failing but he was fighter. From the hospital bed he encouraged me to continue taking care of my body. His struggle with sickle cell disease taught us one thing…the doctors had NO IDEA what to do with him. Since there is no cure for sickle cell anemia the doctors would only be able to treat the symptoms and his pain with drugs. The drugs would ultimately contribute to his organ failure.

My younger sister would also give birth to a baby girl who would have to live with his disease. This sparked an interest in holistic medicines and remedies that could help our bodies to heal and strengthen naturally without pharmaceutical drugs. We realized that while the medical professionals studied for years and were deserving of their respect, we, ultimately were the stewards of our individual bodies.

After being separated for almost a year. Anthony asked me to lunch so that we could talk. He had been doing some soul searching of his own and wanted to apologize for what he called his ignorance. He'd been going to church and was getting counseling once a week with a therapist that helped him realize how important I was to him.

From there we went for a ride. He said he had a surprise for me. We went downtown to the courthouse where he asked me again to marry him. My father was there dressed in a white linen suit and Jesus sandals. He'd already given Anthony his blessing and was there to witness the moment. I said, yes.

Once we were married, we moved into another apartment together. He had not immediately shared the news of our nuptials with his family since a few of them were major contributors to the dysfunction and toxicity in our past. Family had been overly involved in our relationship and he promised things would be different in our marriage.

Two months later I was ready to file for an annulment. I had no evidence of infidelity at this point, but his temper was out of control. He would come home from work upset about something that had nothing to do with me and there was nothing I could do to calm him. It could be something as trivial as the heavy traffic and it was somehow my fault. Somehow, I was the enemy. If his key got stuck in the door or his dinner wasn't freshly made when he walked in the door from work, we would go days without speaking. I just had to wait it out. I'd apologize and take the blame to restore peace. Sometimes it worked, most times it didn't. I was already asking myself, why did I get married. It was more of the same. What was I thinking? Was I thinking at all? I didn't take time to pray about such a huge decision before saying, yes. I reacted based on my emotions at that time. He'd stopped going to church. He'd stopped getting counseling. What once felt like forward movement was now feeling like a train moving backwards to nowhere.

I told Anthony that I would reconsider the annulment if I could speak to his therapist and he needed to diagnose him with something I could understand. Loving a man was not supposed to be this hard. I needed somebody to tell me I wasn't crazy. Help me understand him when he couldn't find the words.

We started going to therapy together. Neither of us wanted the marriage to fail but we didn't know how to make it last. Consulting with family and friends had proven to be a bad idea in the past. It led to people picking sides and passing judgement. We both opened about our childhood traumas. The therapist points out that while I had made a conscious effort to heal and help others find healing, Anthony had not. Deep down he was still that scared little boy with a grown man exterior. He was still sulking in the unfortunate unfolding of his past. Much worse - He had a vision of what he wanted his life to look like. The life that he felt he deserved was not only unrealistic - it was not his reality and he blamed me for it. He felt that I wasn't fitting to his image and he deserved better.

It was hurtful hearing the therapist's interpretation of my husband's innermost thoughts and feelings. Nonetheless he expressed his commitment to making our marriage work. One of his complaints about me was that I was too strong. He wanted me to show more emotion and more vulnerability. He felt that I was more consumed between the salon, the church and with the kids that he felt ignored. The therapist recommended that we take a vacation together. Just the two of us. We would work on being more open and honest with each other about our feeling and we would actively listen while the other is speaking without interrupting each other. This would be a huge step toward strengthening our relationship.

We drove down to Key West for a partial weekend getaway and argued halfway there. I'd packed healthy snacks for the drive. He was instantly upset because I'd only packed one cinnamon bun and when he was hungry, I offered him half. During him reprimanding me for messing up yet again as a wife, he threw the entire thing out of the window and didn't speak to me for the rest of the night.

The next morning, we had a silent breakfast under a cabana near the shore. I'd made reservations for some early morning water excursions with the hotel concierge, but he wasn't in the mood. I called down and rescheduled for the early afternoon departure. By then he had begun to open a little more. We were at least speaking to each other, but I felt it was safe to go out in public with him and not be embarrassed. Whenever he was upset, he didn't care who saw his ugly. He wouldn't need to speak a word. People would just know that he was not to be bothered.

The first leg of our water adventure was parasailing. That was the ice breaker. The rush was so intense he forgot to be upset. Before he knew it, he was smiling. The remainder of the weekend was pleasant after that. We were able to actively practice some of the things recommended by the therapist including restoring our sex life.

We both felt closer after that weekend. When we got back home, I even arranged a lunch with his father in hopes of restoring their relationship. I had a front row seat to witness the effects of my husband not having a relationship with his father and how it ultimately bled into his relationship with our son. I thought that if I could mend their relationship it would help my husband to find healing.

We met at a local Applebee's and I shared my concerns with my father in law. I wanted to know his truth about what happened. so far, I had heard Anthony's version of the story and versions of other members of Anthony's maternal side of the family, but I had never heard his father's side.

He shared with me that they were young when Anthony's mom got pregnant. Their families were close, but the news of her pregnancy created a rift between their mothers. The dysfunction between the two grandmothers ultimately influenced the way the two of them thought of and treated each other. In the middle was this baby boy who never felt a sense of belonging because both his parents married and had other children with their spouses. He told me that he tried to establish a relationship with Anthony. He visited with him on the weekends and they would go to the movies and do things with his family, sometimes eve one on one. After some time, he just stops calling and coming by. They never knew why.

His father had heard from other members of the family that Anthony had spoken ill of him and he'd responded with some negative words of his own further tarnishing the relationship. His willingness to meet up with me was enough for me to believe that he still wanted to have a relationship with his son. I wanted me kids to have a relationship with their grandfather and other members of their family. We arranged for him to cover to our house for dinner and take a step toward doing just that. We would start off without the kids and the two of them would work on fixing their relationship before and get all their words and emotions out before including anyone else.

Anthony was not aware that I was having lunch with his father that day period when I arrived home, I went straight up to him and told him where I'd been and why. I shared with him that things that his father had revealed to me and asked why he hadn't shared these things with me before. Anthony's version of the story was that his father lived in the same neighborhood and he never saw him. He did not have a relationship with most of his siblings, only his brother would speak. How was his dad's version so different? Anthony broke down into tears and confessed that his father said was true. He had been holding the grudge for so long, but it was a grudge based on emotions and untruths. He too was ready to put the past behind him and move forward with his relationship with his father.

Two days before the dinner I received a call from Anthony's father. His wife does not approve of this meeting. She questioned why it had taken so long for Anthony to reach out and why his wife had to do it. She did not agree with our decision to have their initial meeting be alone with just the two of them. Why couldn't she be there?

The conversation was short but loaded. I could tell by his tone that it was already decided. He was not coming. There was nothing I could say or do to persuade his wife to allow him to come. I had a feeling her reasons were deeper than what was explained. She was afraid, but of what?

I was disappointed for my husband. After years of an estranged relationship with his father he was finally ready to speak with him – and now this. He was cancelling because his wife was not happy. I realized that the secrets, the lies, and the history of this family was deeper than my love could reach. While my intentions were pure, I saw that this could easily reopen old wounds and create deeper ones. I would not be a vessel in the enemy's ploy to further destroy my husband. I told Anthony that his father cancelled because his wife wasn't feeling well and never tried to get involved again.

CHAPTER 18

It was a busy day at the salon and my energy was low. I was feeling faint. In the middle of a braiding service I took a moment to lay down on the couch in the office and woke up 30 minutes later. At the end of the day I drove home feeling like death. My body was tired. I made it up the stairs and passed out in the hallway of our apartment. Anthony and his friend helped me into the kids' room where I stayed that night. The kids were visibly worried. I didn't have the strength to comfort them. Instead, they consoled me.

It was the weekend before the 1st day of school. My schedule was booked up from 8am to midnight with a few small breaks in between. I messaged all my clients that were scheduled for the next day. I let them know that I was not feeling well but that I would do my best to keep up with the scheduled service times. I was blessed with great clients, many of them became friends. They were great about taking care of me. They would bring food when they were on their way making sure I had optimal energy to push through the busy weekend.

I pushed through each day successfully, but the drive home would be a struggle. It's when I'd feel all the stress that that I was hiding take over my body all at once. After the third day I went home and vomited. Finally, I asked Anthony to go out and purchase a pregnancy test. I had never felt this way during any of my other pregnancies, but it's been seven years since our daughter was born. I was convinced that I was either pregnant or I was dying.

I was pregnant.

The date of conception indicated that our trip to Key West was more successful than we'd originally thought. I left the positive pregnancy test on the bathroom sink for Anthony to see. As always, he was ecstatic to learn that we had a baby on the way. In his excitement he admitted that he'd been trying to get me pregnant again since we got married. This was disturbing news to me because we hadn't agreed to having another child. We Spoke about it, but I told him that I was happy with the two that we had. If we were to have a third child, I would want to have been married at least 5 years and make sure that our marriage was solid before we bring another child into the situation. We'd both agreed that this was best. We did not have the most active sex life which is one of the concerns he'd brought up during our counseling sessions. But he never communicated that he was trying to have a baby. Perhaps he thought this would buy him more time or strengthen our marriage. It did the opposite. It was the nail in the coffin.

This was the hardest pregnancy yet. Where I'd been vibrant and fully functional through both pregnancies with my other kids, this one felt as if the baby was killing me from the inside. I didn't have an appetite. I was afraid to eat anything because I could barely keep anything down. Even water came back up. Nothing helped. No home remedy, no holistic approach. Even the scent of my favorite perfume sent me running to the toilet. Then I started having muscle spasms in my throat while sleeping. Scariest feeling ever. These were all symptoms I'd never experienced.

My OBGYN that delivered our first two kids had recently retired. I had to find a new one. Since my first two pregnancies had both resulted in preterm births my new OBGYN ordered tests to figure out why. The results indicated that I had an iron deficiency caused by a beta thalassemia trait. It was explained to be a form of sickle cell anemia which is what my father has. That caused my body to reject iron absorption which explained why my energy was so low. The fetus was healthy. Taking all the iron I'd stored up in my body for healthy growth and development of the baby. I needed a nap after simple everyday tasks like vacuuming the floor or grocery shopping. My iron levels were dangerously low. The doctor warned I may need to have a blood transfusion at some point before, during, or after delivering my baby.

My father was shocked to learn of my diagnosis and felt responsible. It was after all something I'd inherited from him. I was thirty years old and pregnant with my third child before learning that I had this disorder. The only thing I could think of that was more miserable than that was having to go through it all alone. My husband could not have been less supportive. I was placed on bedrest for the duration of my pregnancy. A nurse would come by, check my vitals and administer a weekly progesterone shot into my butt. Against the doctor's orders I was still taking clients, but I was working less hours and scheduling breaks in between each appointment. Closer to time for me to deliver I took and early maternity leave, but I was still taking a few clients at home.

I wasn't bringing in the same amount of money now that I was working less. The financial burden fell mostly on Anthony. I was only able to pay my car note and cover other expenses like groceries and odd things around the house. Having to carry our family financially was weighing heavily on our marriage. We'd stopped going to counseling after finding out we were pregnant. Now is when we needed therapy more than ever. I began to sense that same resentment that was so evident before. Anthony was next to me in the bed while on the phone with another woman. I could hear her asking him if they could have lunch later. His response was that he could make it because he was working on another side of town that day. Not because he was a married mand and it was disrespectful to his marriage and to his wife.

I decided at that moment that I was done. I was going to give it three months after the baby is born and then I was leaving him. I didn't have the energy to fight for it anymore. It would take some divine intervention to get me to stay. I wasn't going to do this anymore.

Our second Daughter was born the day after our first daughter's 8th birthday. we could not even celebrate our daughter's birthday completely because I'd started having Braxton Hicks contractions. Our first nights at home were measurable because the baby was not yet sleeping at night. I was still going through health issues of my own. on top of that I'd still have to get up and get our older 2 kids to and from school. I had no help with any of this. our baby was not even a week old and I would have to take her out every day to the school to wait in car line for dismissal.

My husband would come home upset because dinner wasn't ready, and the house was a mess. Asking him to keep an eye on the kids while I take a shower would result in an argument of its own. In his mind I had been home doing nothing all day.

After the first month I resumed taking clients at home. This proved to be an almost impossible task because my breast-fed baby only wanted to be held all day. She could not be consult by anyone else and would cry for hours on end. Instead of picking her up every time she cried, I would let her learn to self sooth. This made Anthony upset because he didn't want to come home to all the noise. He would take his time getting home from work just to avoid the whole scene. There were times when I'd work half the day at the salon and then still take a client or two at home. A close friend from church came over to receive a simple service. I was embarrassed that she had to witness my husband at his worse. I'd asked her to meet me at the house so that I could relieve Anthony who had been home all day with the kids. It was late. We were both tired. But Paula was someone who was close to our family and she was only getting a ponytail. I didn't think it would be a problem. She felt the tension in the air even before he started going off and she offered to leave. I asked her to stay, afraid of what might happen after she left. This was not his norm. He's usually more reserved when company was around. I thought I'd just stall the service. He'd just go outside and smoke and then go to sleep waiting for my company to leave. He didn't.

Paula, I need to have a conversation with my wife for a minute.

No, you don't. This won't take long at all and then we can talk but I'm not doing this with you right now."

"I can leave." Paula proceeded to get up and slowly make her departure.

"Yes, please leave." Anthony said.

I told her, "No, it's okay you can stay."

You sure? I don't want no problems. She was halfway to the front door.

I directed my attention to Anthony. "I'm not arguing with you right now.

Can we do this later?" Later never came. He shouted a few obscenities stumbling over his words not sure what he was upset about and then went outside to smoke. I pretended not to be bothered but I was on the edge of a breakdown. My energy had been depleted beyond my iron deficiency. My spirit was weak. I didn't have any more fight left in me. Before leaving, Paula was genuinely concerned and asked me if I'd be okay tonight.

"I'll be fine." I told her. She'd heard stories about his temper, but she had just witnessed it for herself. I'd downplayed just how scary it was in person. I think everyone wanted to believe he wasn't capable of such rage. He was very good at making himself for the public. He worked hard to maintain his image. There were parts of himself that he'd rather keep hidden from the world. People only saw a charming, chivalrous, humble family man which what is exactly he wanted them to see. People loved him. I never wanted to expose his demons, I wanted to help him to heal from them. Exposing his demons would only open the door for outsiders to judge my husband and our marriage.

We slept in separate rooms. I'd been sleeping on the couch since finding out my husband was again entertaining the company of other women. I'd started taking classes online to finish my degree program at FIU. Now that the baby was born, her bassinet was set up next to the couch. I needed to get her on a sleeping schedule so that I could study and take care of the other priorities around the house and with the other kids. Anthony would come out of the room in the middle of the night. He'd be upset that I was sleeping while the baby was crying, or I was awake and letting herself sooth. I wouldn't pick her up right away. It disturbed his rest. We'd argue about why his rest was more important than mine. I felt that he had such unrealistic expectations of me. His expectation were things that no woman could juggle all alone. He somehow expected me to make the impossible happen. I tried to get him to see that he was being irrational but to no avail.

A christening is a ritual symbolizing dedicating a child to God. The child is blessed by the elders of the church and surrounded by loved ones. Anthony knew all about this practice. Our other two kids had been christened as well and he was present for both. He knew that this was an important occasion but somehow hoped he would be required to participate this time. I was getting the kids groomed and dressed. He was laying down in the bed not making any moves to get dressed himself. It was not at all unusual for him to lay around while I took care of the kids and then wait until minutes before we needed to leave out of the house before getting up. This time he didn't get up at all.

"Are you going to get dressed, Anthony?"

"For what?" He was doing the stupid dumb face again. The face he makes when he's trying to come up with some lame justification for whatever he's about to say or do. The face he makes when he's hoping that I buy into whatever dumb thing he's about to say – but he knows it's not very likely.

After an exchange of words, he did get up to shower and get dressed for the service. It was hard to ignore the disgruntled look that was all over his face. He was letting everyone know that he didn't want to be there. It was such a distraction. People were asking me if everything was okay

I prayed about leaving my husband. I didn't want to displease God, but it wasn't God who told me to marry him in the first place. I had made that decision on my own. My life reflected the choices I'd made. I was living with the consequences (and rewards) of the actions I'd chosen. In a dream I could clearly hear God's voice say, "continue to show him love."

But can I DIVORCE him though? God never answered that question directly.

I was obedient to the command from God and I continued to show love to my husband despite how it made me feel. Whenever I made dinner, I'd offered him some and make him a plate even if he didn't eat it. Often, he would know that I'm making dinner and would pick up fast food on the way home just to spite me. He hardly ever refused breakfast. Sometimes I would fix his plate, but I wouldn't deliver it to him. He'd have to come to the kitchen to get it himself. Every week when I did the laundry, I'd wash his clothes – but I wouldn't fold them. Perhaps I wasn't entirely obedient to the command after all.

I made lunch for him and delivered it out to him at work. In the back of my mind I was hoping to catch him and whoever she was. I would throw the whole sandwich in his face and head straight to the courthouses. Instead I was greeted with gratitude. He had not eaten anything all day and was hungry.

Our baby hadn't yet completely conformed to a sleeping pattern, but I was eager to get back into the salon. I hired a young lady from my church to babysit for me. I scheduled clients with large breaks in between so that I could go home and nurse. I'd also take some clients at home whenever possible. I was trying my best to get back to life as it was before. Every day was a reminder that those days were gone.

The cost of paying the babysitter grew to be more than I could handle on my own. I was limited on the number of hours that I could spend at the salon with having to juggle my duties as a mother and wife. I started my workdays at 8am. I needed to nurse or pump my breastmilk every 2-3 hours. I could not take any clients after 2pm because I needed to leave out at 3pm to pick up my older kids from school by 3:30pm. I was juggling homework help with preparing dinner. My husband doesn't eat leftovers, so I didn't have the luxury of cooking a big meal and eating off it for a couple of days. There was more money going out than what was coming in.

I asked my husband to help. I needed to be able to work more hours. He was reluctant but agreed to keeping the kids only on Friday and Saturday nights so that I could work later and make more money. Friday night he left work and went to relieve the babysitter of her duties. My phone probably rang every hour. Either he was calling to ask me how much longer I'd be at work or the kids were calling to say they were hungry. There was a food truck outside the salon that day, so I left the salon and took dinner to them at home. When I arrived home, the house was a mess. The evidence of what the kids had been eating was all throughout the living room. Doritos and Honey Buns. The baby was asleep which meant she was off her sleep schedule and would be up all night. I'd left three 6oz bottles for the baby and told him to feed her every 2-3 hours. He'd gone through all three bottles of breastmilk in just a few hours because she kept crying. She wasn't crying because she was hungry but feeding her until she fell asleep was easier than hearing the screams and finding other way to try to soothe her. I couldn't be picky though; I'd asked Anthony to stay home with the kids and he was doing what I asked him to do. I wanted so badly to complain. I couldn't both work at the salon and oversee what was happening at home. I needed him to share the responsibilities with me. I'd have the conversation with him another time. I decided this was not the time to fight that battle. I'd give him some time to adjust on his own.

That time would never come. By his second day on the job he'd already had enough. Saturday was a longer day of daddy duties which meant he'd be alone with the kids for hours. I did take a two-hour lunch break and took food to them at home. I was able to allow him to get a nap while I nurse the baby. It gave him some relief. I thought I was doing the right thing knowing I'd be working late into the night and knowing the maintenance involved with the routine I'd established for with our kids. They were accustomed to a lot of attention and hands on involvement. Anthony was accustomed to not having to be involved at all. This was a transition for all of us.

Saturday night ran a bit later than anticipated. I told Anthony that I'd be working until around 9pm. The salon can be unpredictable though and it's easy to get caught up in time especially when money is the focus. I didn't finish until around midnight. I arrived home to a very unhappy husband. He was visibly upset but I didn't have the energy for a verbal altercation. The kids were still awake. Everyone was in front of the television including baby girl. I told the kids to go to bed and went straight into the shower before going to my bed on the couch.

Anthony started blasting dance hall music from the bedroom. He saw that I was tired and was determined to disturb my rest that night. I just didn't want to fight. After a while I got up and closed the bedroom door to drown out some of the noise. He forcefully pulled the door open so hard that the doorknob collided with the wall leaving a big hole.

"Can you please just turn the music down; Anthony I'm trying to sleep."

He ignored me as I stood there in the doorway. It was now around 1am and he was being childish. Not only was it annoying but if one of the neighbors were to call the police, we could get evicted for violating our least agreement. I reached in and closed the door again. His response was the same. He snatched the door back open.

"Don't touch my door again." He warned. I gave him the reaction he was looking for. Let's argue.

"Your door? I live here too."

"You can go. You serve no purpose here anyway. You're worthless"

"I'm not going anywhere. You can't even manage the kids for two days without calling me a thousand times because you can't handle parenting your own kids. You feed them bullshit all day. It looks like you haven't changed the baby's diaper since I did it when I came home on my lunch break. But I'm worthless????"

"You've been using me for the past 10 months and using the baby as an excuse to be lazy and not work. Yes, you're worthless."

"You know what I'm tired of this. Let's just go down to the courthouse together on Monday and get a divorce. First thing Monday Morning I want to be there when the doors open up." The "D" word must've struck a chord with him. He had the same look of rage in his eyes that I'd seen just before things would get physical. He was in front of me staring into my eyes when he said,

"The only way we're getting a divorce if death do you part." He said it twice. The second time was scarier than the first and I believed him.

It didn't make any sense to me why he would want to stay in a marriage with someone he felt so negatively about. I'm worthless. I could leave. I serve no purpose. I was using him. But he didn't want a divorce. He didn't want a divorce and thought threatening me would make me stay. I decided not to sleep on the couch that night. I was adamant about wanting the divorce and I took his threat to my life seriously. I slept in the kids' room with the door locked.

The next day was a Sunday. I continued with my usual Sunday routine beginning with church service. He was already awake and sitting on the foot of the bed when I walked into the room to shower and get dressed.

"I'm sorry." He said. "I did it again." He was referring to losing himself and his temper. Going too far. It was rare that he'd apologize for anything. I wanted to believe him. The threat to my life in connection with calling me lazy and worthless. Telling me to get out. I believed this was how he really felt. These were all the things he'd been holding back. I believe he meant what he said, he was only sorry that he'd spoken the words instead of keeping them in his head. Regardless, it had been showing in his actions toward me for quite some time. The therapist had warned me that he could snap because his expectations versus reality were so unrealistic.

I didn't respond. I proceeded to take a shower and get ready for church. During service I couldn't think of anything other than the things he said to me. They kept repeating over and over in my head. I'd mastered smiling like everything was okay, so no one suspected that anything was wrong. After church, the kids and I returned home. Anthony had cleaned up the house and was doing laundry. I kept my distance and remained silent. For the remainder of the day we didn't speak any words to each other. That night I dreamt my husband killed me.

I woke up the next morning and meditated deeply on my life and the choices I'd made. This isn't love. This isn't how I want to live my life. If I didn't leave, if I remained in this dysfunctional and toxic relationship, If I didn't get out now my marriage could very well end in death. My death. I didn't know what my husband was capable of. I don't even thing HE really knew what he was capable of. But I wasn't about to stick around any longer to find out. I packed enough clothes for myself and the kids to get by for a few days and we left while he was at work. My friend, Paula, allowed us to stay at her house for a couple of months while I applied for permission to leave the state. The only family I had that was willing and able to take me in with my kids was my sister in Alabama.

The judge denied my request to leave the state and my request for a restraining order against my husband because I'd only asked the he be kept away from me temporarily – not forever. I believed it was unrealistic to ask for a forever restraining order since we shared three kids together. I didn't want to restrict his access to the kids and I surely didn't want to put more people in our business than necessary. I just wanted him to stay away from me until he got some help. The judge, however, took that as an indicator that I was not really in fear for my life and he denied my request.

Anthony responded by contacting child protective services claiming that the kids were in possible danger. He knew that I had no money and nowhere to go. I wasn't sure if he was trying to take have the kids taken away from me or if this was an extreme measure, he'd take to try to get me to come home. Based on previous experiences of our years together in an on again off again relationship I knew that this wasn't about his concern for the welfare of our kids. He knew that I would protect my kids with my life if it ever came down to it. I believed he was more upset that he didn't know where I was rather than concern about where the children were. The kids were not being kept away from him. I'd only asked that he stay away from ME. He knew that they were safe, and he knew how to access them if he wanted to. I never changed their school which was only a half mile from where he resided. I even told him that he could pick the kids up from school anytime he wanted to and keep them overnight. Whatever his motive, it didn't work. Instead, the social worker offered resources on government assistance. I could qualify to get childcare services so that I could work and get back on my feet. After interviewing the kids at school, she contacted me to see our living arrangements. She saw that the kids were safe and well taken care of. I would never put my kids in harm's way. She also recommended a mediator to help Anthony and I figure out how to co-parent together throughout the situation. We never did follow up on that lead.

CHAPTER 19

"People are often unreasonable irrational and self-centered. Forgive them anyway. If you are kind, people may accuse you of ulterior motives. Be kind anyway. If you are honest people may cheat you. Be honest anyway. If you find happiness, people may be jealous. Be happy anyway. The good you do today, will be forgotten tomorrow. Do good anyway. Give the world the best you have, and it may never be enough. Give your best anyway. For you see, in the end, it is between you and God. It was never between you and them anyway."

– Mother Theresa

Months passed and I was struggling to maintain a sense of normalcy in our lives when my father fell sick again. The baby was having trouble sleeping at night. A sleep study showed that she would stop breathing for up to 3 minutes at a time throughout the night. For three minutes she was not getting any oxygen to her brain. She was diagnosed with sever sleep apnea. Before scheduling surgery, the ENT wanted to try a holistic approach and see if her body could heal itself. We changed her diet and closely monitored the weather during allergy season. I was suffering migraines more frequently and experiencing hair loss trying to manage all the stress. I continued the routine with the kids. Our son had basketball practice almost every other day and our oldest daughter had dance practice, recitals etc. I didn't want to take them away from the things that distracted them the most. These things gave them an escape.

I took a break from serving in ministry at my church. I couldn't commit myself to the responsibility of lead servant when my life was in shambles. Some would say that serving in ministry should have been my escape, but it was the opposite. I was falling apart. Being in leadership meant you had to hold it together and that just wasn't my reality. It was becoming increasingly hard to smile through the storm going on in my life. By now news of my troubled marriage had started to spread around the church. People knew my personal business and did would offer their unsolicited opinions about what I should and should not do with my life. The same people who had fellowshipped with me over the years seemed to be happy to have a front row seat to my struggles. There were people who knew the most intimate details of my separation with my husband, only it wasn't myself that had shared this information with them. The people closest to me were discussing my private family matters for others to judged. When people would ask me how I'm doing and offer to pray for my family, I did not believe the prayers were genuine. Many of those that were offering to pray simply did not have my best interest at heart. I didn't know who to trust. I couldn't tell the difference between those that genuinely wanted well and those who were secretly rejoicing in my calamity and praying for my downfall. I couldn't trust anyone to help me without them telling other people that they'd helped me. Church gossip, whether it was about me, changed the way I viewed the very people I'd grow to call my friends. I started refusing help from everyone.

Despite what I was feeling I knew that leaving my husband was not going to be an easy task. I was going to have to climb this mountain alone. While there were many that seemed to want to help me stay in that dark place, there were a select few angels in my life that did not need to know they details. They didn't need an update on the newest drama every time we spoke. They genuinely wanted to see me elevated to a place of higher energy. I didn't feel judged. Instead of asking, "how is everything with you and Anthony?" I'd hear, "hey why don't you bring the kids by for dinner so you can get some rest." That's all I ever really needed.

I never quite understood church hurt before this. I was in a dark place.

My spirit was weak. My life was falling apart. Both my father and my baby were sick. Every thought in my head was so loud to me. I wanted to scream. I wanted to tell everyone that had an opinion about my life and my marriage to go to hell. I wanted to say, fuck you all – but that wasn't very Christian like. It was hard for me to see anything beyond what I was going through.

My father passed away on the morning of my son's 11th birthday. I had been at the hospital by his side in ICU all night along with his wife and my other siblings. He was on life support; he wasn't doing so well. I held his hand and whispered, "I love you" in his ear knowing he'd hear me. The doctors were telling us that he wouldn't make it through the night. He had been hospitalized many times before, but he always came home. This time felt different. I stayed as late as I could, but it was well past midnight, I had to get back to my kids. They were staying with my son's godparents. They insisted that we stay overnight instead of waking up the kids and driving home at such a late hour. I'm glad they did. I got the call that morning after sleeping only a few hours. His wife was wailing, "He's GONE!" on the other end of my phone. My son's godmother heard me crying and came to take my phone away from my ear. She urged me to go to him. She would make sure that my son enjoyed his birthday. Because of them, his birthday would not be just a sad reminder of the day grandpa died. I arrived at the hospital just in time to see them place a tag on his toe. He was cold. I kissed his forehead as they zipped him up into a black body bag. They transferred his body from the hospital bed onto what looked like a metal table with wheels. I couldn't even take much time to grieve. I was numb. As much as I wanted to scream out loud, I had to be strong for my kids who were very close to him. I found both sadness and joy in the last conversation I had with my father. He said he was ready to go home. He wasn't referring to his home here on earth. He wasn't afraid. He had lived much longer than the doctors expected. When the doctors had said that he would not be able to have children, he was a father to 12. His strength gave me the strength I needed to pick up the pieces and move forward through my own personal storm. After my father's funeral I isolated myself away from everyone including my closest friends. I decided to make my mental health more of a priority over my friendships and relationships.

I found a nice 2-bedroom apartment at an affordable price in a quiet neighborhood and made it our home. When I first inquired about renting a unit in this community, I was told that there was a 2 year wait list. I put my name on the wait list and continued my search once again feeling hopeless. This was in December, just a week or so before my dad passed away. Midway through January I received a call that a unit was available for me to move in in February. Those that were on the waitlist ahead of me had either found another residence or could not qualify to rent. That 2-year waiting list shortened to 2 months just like that. My mind was blown. This was divine intervention. That was a mountain I could not have moved on my own. I moved into my apartment with only our clothes and the kids' bunkbeds. The quiet, empty space was a perfect chance to start over.

I was able to get daycare assistance through the resource provided by my case worker. I'd just started working as the Office Manager of my friends' Pediatric Therapy Clinic again, but I was moving into my new apartment only a little over a month after getting the job. I gave up the salon and was now working at the clinic full time, but I wasn't making enough money to afford aftercare for my older kids. I tried working part time, but I could not afford to pay my bills and take care of three kids on part time pay. I would use my lunch hour to drive across town and pick up my kids from school. My back was against the wall. Every step forward seemed to result in either a stop signs or being knocked backwards.

I was still taking my college courses online which offered me the flexibility that I needed to juggle school, work, and three kids. I was taking clients at home to make up for the difference between my monthly expenses and what I earned working part time at the clinic. People ask me how I did it. I can't answer that, but I didn't do it all alone. I just kept waking up. I kept moving. Instead of wallowing in self-pity and giving up on life, I put one foot in front of the other. We had everything we needed. I had to push pause on the kids' after school activities unless I could get a clone. They were not happy about this at all, but I hoped they'd one day understand.

After my divorce was final, I needed to spend some alone time with God. My Pastor would say that sometimes isolation was necessary for elevation. He was right. More than anything I needed that time one-on-one with God. That was the best thing I could have ever done for myself. Protecting my peace. I was unapologetically willing to lose my friends and my social status if the contrary meant losing my mind. I was getting to know him on a deeper level and learning to love myself again.

I stopped going to church (the building) and began reading the bible on my own. I did not, however, limit my reading to the teachings and the stories of the bible. Iyanla Vanzant's "One Day my Soul Just Opened Up" several times before but each time I received it differently being at different stages of my life. The Alchemist, Who Says You Can't You Do, and The Four Agreements were some other self-help books I'd indulged when I first began. I was praying and fasting and then I learned the significance of silencing my thoughts through meditation and stillness. I was intentional about my quiet time and protecting my peace. For years I'd placed limits on God and to Christian beliefs, but God is so much bigger. There's so much knowledge beyond the pages of the bible. God sends His messages by angels of many languages. Messages of peace and love and how to walk in your purpose. The bible is one of many manuscripts translating these messages. There are other message and messengers all around us, guiding us. This lead me to a more intimate and a more personal relationship with God. I was that little girl again finding comfort in the arms of my Heavenly Father.

My spiritual understanding started to evolve along with my spiritual beliefs as I investigated some of the different philosophies and practices of the world. I started to define truth for myself and investigate what had been fed to me as truth. I read books on Buddhism, the Dalai Lama, a Persian philosopher, Baha u Llah, Desmond Tutu, The Mayans, Aztecs, and Babylonians. I already knew how to fast and participated in a yearly fast with other members of my church, but a renewed spirit enabled me to understand and embrace the concept of fasting on a deeper level.

I practiced finding inner peace through Falun Dafa. Spiritual enlightening enabled me to see myself in others and a sight beyond what I'd seen with the naked eye. I was able to see people's soul. I felt their energy. I learned how powerful my thoughts were and how they'd contributed to how I've treated myself in the past and how I'd allowed others to treat me. My dreams became more vivid as well as the messages I received through prayer and meditation.

I stopped looking at myself as a victim and held myself accountable for my contributions to how my life had unfolded. This pivot point in my life taught me to appreciate the good along with the bad. While there are many things we can control, like what we manifest through our thoughts and actions and the love we show ourselves. There will always be those things we simply can't control like the weather. We can't control other people. We can only control ourselves. When faced with adversity you can choose how you respond. How you respond reflects how you feel.

I learned to love myself flaws and all. The hardest part about spiritual awakening is having that honest talk with yourself. Confronting my own demons and purging all the self-defeating thoughts and actions I'd become so familiar with. I had to unlearn and learn to never stop learning. Never stop growing. Never stop.

I feel compassion for those that are stuck in the prisons of their minds. I forgave my abusers and over time I learned to forgive myself for allowing the abuse. I forgave myself for not walking in my truth. I forgave myself for the years of insecurities and self-doubt. For being afraid to walk in my own light. It takes a significant amount of courage to tell yourself the truth. To allow yourself to feel the pain of your brokenness. But the response to that, beyond the pain, is healing and freedom from that bondage.

I still struggle with totally forgiving my mother. She's still battling demons of her own. I don't hate her, I love her, but I no longer try to force a relationship with her. I don't have a yearning for her love anymore. If she ever needs anything from me and I have the means, I'm there. I've accepted that she is who she is, and it was not my responsibility to try to change her. I would focus my energy on healing myself without her. On being the loving mother, I remembered her to be when I was in elementary school. My children know her as their grandmother but the distance between us and in our relationship spilled over into her relationship with my kids. I don't fully trust her to be a part of our village. Call me Mama Bear but I will never knowingly place my kids under her unsupervised care. For a while I thought of it as shielding my kids from experiencing the same mistreatment, hurt and toxicity of who she is. I do, however, wish I could. I would love for my kids to have a grandmother that gave them things like love, time, wisdom, history and tradition, and helped produce balanced well-rounded kids. Over the years she and I both made several attempts at a band aid solution for our relationship without dealing with the core of the problem. She stayed at my home for a week after my second daughter was born. She went and complained to one of my sisters that she was miserable the entire time because there was no food in my house. I ate too healthy. I did practice healthy eating but when I knew she was coming I asked her what she'd like me to get for her from the grocery store. She said she was fine and would eat whatever was there. Once she arrived, I again offered to make a trip to the grocery store for her. She said she was fine. I was shocked to hear otherwise. I would do things like giving her a makeover and taking her out for her birthday – things she expressed that she enjoyed. Later I'd hear her express that she never enjoyed these things at all. I'm afraid that my truth would hurt her deeply. I don't want to be a reason for her to shed tears, so things were left unsaid.

My pain had purpose. When clients would sit in my chair at the salon it was like a therapy session. I was blessed to have clients that trusted me with their innermost secrets. Through my experiences and the knowledge, I had attained I was able to speak life into these women who often felt as if life was swallowing them alive and tell them that I've been there. There were occasions when the person in my chair would instead pour into ME and lift ME up.

My marriage was over, and I had no desire to try again to fix what was broken. I still believed that we could raise our kids tighter without having to share a bed together to keep the peace. It was important to me that our kids had both parents active and involved in their lives. This would not come easily to Anthony. It took him a while before he'd even begin to comprehend a place of selfless love and putting what was best for the kids ahead of his own ego. I gave up on trying to be friends for sake of the kids. It always backfired. When he wasn't taking me for granted, he was transferring all the parental responsibilities over to me for his own convenience. He would mistake my kindness and willingness to work together as flirtation or as a sign that there may be a chance that we'd reconnect romantically for some sex with the ex. That was the farthest thing from my mind. I felt it was important for us to find a way to get along as co-parents solely because I believed it was what was best for the kids. He'd get upset and reverted to childish behaviors whenever I rejected his advances. It got to the point where he was no longer welcome inside my home. He would stand outside, and the kids would go outside to greet him. He needed more time to come to grips with what was reality and what he'd created in his head.

During my last semester of school one of my classes required me to take a test that was supposed to tell me what career field I be most productive and find most fulfilling. The results revealed that I would make a great teacher. I disagreed. I majored in Business Administration. My entire work history had been in service and finance. Even before the salon I'd spent 7 years in Banking. I shared this with one of my coworkers as a joke. I didn't expect her response to be what it was. She had just been offered a job at the school where her kids attended but she turned it down due to her family circumstances. She agreed with the test and thought I'd make a great teacher. This reminded me of the time my Pastor thought I'd make a great member of the First Friends Ministry and it turned out to be a most rewarding experience. He saw something in me that I didn't see in myself. I felt the same way about Anna. Teaching could very well be my next ministry. I inquired with the Principal at my kids' school about substituting and the rest is history. My first-year teaching was much like what I'd expected when dealing with other people's kids. I had covered a fifth-grade class during my time as a substitute and quickly learned that Elementary school was not for me. I'm not sure if it was the non-stop questions about my weave – I was wearing faux locs - or the kid that told me he thinks he pooped his pants on the stairs. It was a no for me.

I loved teaching math middle school students. This was a crucial time in their transition from babies to adolescents. Having the spirit to want to help everyone, I was still working on setting boundaries. I don't always know when to say, "no" and when to let go. I knew it would be easy for me to grow attached to my students and their stories, so I prayed. I prayed that I would not get too attached. I didn't want to be the teacher that students trusted with all their problems because I knew I'd be limited on what I could do about it. I wanted to help, but I could not get involved. It was a struggle to find a balance that didn't conflict with my own optimism. I would find myself mentoring the young ladies when I noticed their desperate attempts for validation. I saw myself in every one of my students, even the once that were a challenge – I saw that there was fear behind their behaviors.

"Children learn more from what you are than what you teach." - W.E.B Du Boise

I took a tough love approach to teaching mush like my parenting style. My students the structure a little more than my biological kids who thought of me to be a bit hard and overprotective at times. Motivation Mondays was time taken away from formulas and proofs and directed toward building students' confidence and self-esteem. Many of the students, for so long, had been told that they were no good at math. Many of them had circumstances beyond their control going on at home that was either a distraction from their learning or their families could not afford tutoring services for them to perform better. Boosting their confidence, speaking to the students like human beings with feelings proved to have a significant impact on the way that they performed. My students would always be shocked to hear me say that I wasn't always good at math. Back in Middle school I received my first F and it was in Algebra. It wasn't until college that I started to make the connections and learned to appreciate math as a language. I encouraged them to be patient with themselves. I only want your best effort every day when you enter my class. I expected them to try. The politics of our school and our education system would not allow much time for me to do Motivation Mondays as a routine by year two.

I would start up a tutoring service that would offer individualized tutoring and small group tutoring at a reduced rate. Eventually I would expand to a non-profit sector that offers free tutoring to qualifying families because everyone deserves a chance. In my first two years of teaching I saw firsthand the disadvantages of those students that needed additional help and their families simply could not afford it.

I don't allow my students to give up on themselves. All around them are excuses and reasons why that would be an easier option. One of the reasons that I push my students is because I want them to know that no matter what side of things you come from the universe will always provide opportunities. You have the ability and power to do what you desire – IF you desire.

When I find myself wanting to complain I'd remind myself of all the times I was afraid before and it always worked out. It didn't always work out the way I wanted it to but somehow it always came together to perfectly align with my purpose. God would always provide whether it was a means to sustain or a means to escape. I learned to see God's hand working behind the scenes. I remember someone said, "God, I don't know what you're doing, but YOU know."

I've embraced my past including the calamity and people that contributed to my growth. It all has purpose. I'm grateful that The Most High God intervened and did not allow those suicidal thoughts and unsuccessful attempts to end my life. I'm glad my story didn't end there. I would have missed out on beautiful opportunities to enjoy the gift of life. There are times I still struggle with forgiving myself for mistakes I'd made in my past. The guilt would eat away at me and I would feel like I'd failed as a mother. It was easy to forgive myself for the things that only affected me, but any loving mother would consider how her decisions affect her kids. My oldest, my son, witnessed the most of the disfunction and toxicity of my past. I imagine it must have left some emotional scars. Even in doing what I thought was best for him, my decisions made it harder for him. When I have these thoughts, I remind myself that I can't change the past. I can only do better moving forward. I keep moving even when I don't always feel up to it. "The butterfly does not look back at the caterpillar in shame, just as you should not look back at your past in shame. Your past was part of your own transformation."

Be patient with yourself. Allow yourself to make some mistakes but don't dwell there. Pick yourself up and realize that it's YOU. You have everything you need within you to find healing and to manifest the desires of your heart. Calamities happen. They can stop you only if you allow it. When they do happen, instead of asking, "Why Me?" Ask yourself, "Why NOT me?" Why can't I be great? Why can't I heal? Why can't I move past the things that held me bound? Why can't I do better, be better, focus better? The answer is – You can!

www.ingramcontent.com/pod-product-compliance
Lightning Source LLC
Chambersburg PA
CBHW050640160426
43194CB00010B/1743